Liberty's Legacy

Our Celebration of The Northwest Ordi~ and The United States Constitution

This exhibition is an important part of the
1987-88 Big Ten University's national bicentennial
commemoration and is sponsored by

Indiana University
Michigan State University
University of Minnesota
Purdue University
University of Illinois
The University of Michigan
Northwestern University
The Ohio State University
University of Wisconsin

And

The Lilly Library,
  Indiana University
The Clements Library,
  University of Michigan
The Newberry Library,
  Chicago
The Ohio Historical Society
The State Historical Society
  of Wisconsin
The Minnesota Historical
  Society

Liberty's Legacy:
Our Celebration of
the Northwest Ordinance and
The United States Constitution

Coordinating Committee

Co-Directors

Frank B. Jones, Indiana University
Gary C. Ness, Ohio Historical Society

Members

William R. Cagle, Indiana University
Mary Helm, Indiana University
Donn M. Coddington, Minnesota Historical Society
John C. Dann, University of Michigan
Dennis East, Ohio Historical Society
William Crowley, State Historical Society of Wisconsin
John Parker, University of Minnesota
Mary Wyly, The Newberry Library

Catalog Editor: Howard Peckham

Catalog Design: Design Communications, Inc.
                Columbus, Ohio

Exhibit Coordinator: Dennis East, Ohio Historical Society

Exhibit Design: Charles B. Froom/Design Associates
                Brooklyn, New York

Exhibit Preparator: Bruce Baby, Ohio Historical Society

Photography: David R. Barker, Ohio Historical Society

Public Lecturers: Charlene N. Bickford and Kenneth R. Bowling
                  George Washington University

Manuscript Typist: Jane Goldsberry, Ohio Historical Society

Typesetting: Dwight Yaeger, Typographer
             Columbus, Ohio

LIBERTY'S LEGACY is officially recognized by the Commission
on the Bicentennial of the United States Constitution.

ISBN 0-87758-020-0
Published by The Ohio Historical Society

Table of Contents

Foreword

Viewers of the exhibit and readers of the catalog will quickly recognize the national significance of this unprecedented assemblage of our documentary heritage. LIBERTY'S LEGACY: OUR CELEBRATION OF THE NORTHWEST ORDINANCE AND UNITED STATES CONSTITUTION is the product of a three year collaborative and cooperative effort of six prestigious universities and historical societies. It is a once in a lifetime feat to gather and to present publicly such an array of significant, original and valuable historical documents.

The gathering of historical documents, maps writings, and illustrations for LIBERTY'S LEGACY will have different meanings to those who view the exhibit and read the catalog. This is as it should be. The historical materials assembled here help elucidate the ideas and ideals and explain the events and results that shaped our national and regional history in the early years of the new nation. Through this presentation, others will come away with an appreciation and pride in our heritage as Americans and Midwesterners.

The hours of researching, selecting, writing, editing, and designing involved here can only be estimated—and admired. The cooperative spirit, the personal and institutional pride and the patience demonstrated by the participants contributed immeasurably to the success of the undertaking. We all owe a debt of gratitude to the staff and trustees of the participating institutions for their contributions. The continuing dedication and diligence of these libraries and historical societies to acquire, preserve, and make available our documentary heritage is equally significant.

LIBERTY'S LEGACY is also an eloquent symbol of the strong commitment of government and the private sector to celebrate the bicentennials of the Northwest Ordinance and the United States Constitution and to support the universities and the state historical societies which preserve our heritage. This exhibition was made possible by grants from the National Endowment for the Humanities, the Lilly Endowment, Inc., the Commission on the Bicentennial of the United States Constitution, the Trustees of Indiana University, the George and Frances Ball Foundation, and the John W. Anderson Foundation. Grants from the National Endowment for the Humanities and the Lilly Endowment, Inc. made publication of this exhibition catalog possible.

The vision and enthusiasm of Frank B. Jones, retired Executive Director of the Indiana University Alumni Association and Director of the Big Ten University project, deserves special recognition in this celebration of the bicentennial of the Northwest Ordinance and the United States Constitution.

Dennis East
Ohio Historical Society

An Ordinance for the Government of the Territory of the United States, North-West of the River Ohio.

BE IT ORDAINED by the United States in Congress assembled, That the said territory, for the purposes of temporary government, be one district; subject, however, to be divided into two districts, as future circumstances may, in the opinion of Congress, make it expedient.

Be it ordained by the authority aforesaid, That the estates both of resident and non-resident proprietors in the said territory, dying intestate, shall descend to, and be distributed among their children, and the descendants of a deceased child in equal parts; the descendants of a deceased child or grand-child, to take the share of their deceased parent in equal parts among them: And where there shall be no children or descendants, then in equal parts to the next of kin, in equal degree; and among collaterals, the children of a deceased brother or sister of the intestate, shall have in equal parts among them their deceased parents share; and there shall in no case be a distinction between kindred of the whole and half blood; saving in all cases to the widow of the intestate, her third part of the real estate for life, and one third part of the personal estate; and this law relative to descents and dower, shall remain in full force until altered by the legislature of the district. —————— And until the governor and judges shall adopt laws as herein after mentioned, estates in the said territory may be devised or bequeathed by wills in writing, signed and sealed by him or her, in whom the estate may be, (being of full age) and attested by three witnesses; —— and real estates may be conveyed by lease and release, or bargain and sale, signed, sealed, and delivered by the person being of full age, in whom the estate may be, and attested by two witnesses, provided such wills be duly proved, and such conveyances be acknowledged, or the execution thereof duly proved, and be recorded within one year after proper magistrates, courts, and registers shall be appointed for that purpose; and personal property may be transferred by delivery, saving, however, to the French and Canadian inhabitants, and other settlers of the Kaskaskies, Saint Vincent's, and the neighbouring villages, who have heretofore professed themselves citizens of Virginia, their laws and customs now in force among them, relative to the descent and conveyance of property.

Be it ordained by the authority aforesaid, That there shall be appointed from time to time, by Congress, a governor, whose commission shall continue in force for the term of three years, unless sooner revoked by Congress; he shall reside in the district, and have a freehold estate therein, in one thousand acres of land, while in the exercise of his office.

There shall be appointed from time to time, by Congress, a secretary, whose commission shall continue in force for four years, unless sooner revoked, he shall reside in the district, and have a freehold estate therein, in five hundred acres of land, while in the exercise of his office; it shall be his duty to keep and preserve the acts and laws passed by the legislature, and the public records of the district, and the proceedings of the governor in his executive department; and transmit authentic copies of such acts and proceedings, every six months, to the secretary of Congress: There shall also be appointed a court to consist of three judges, any two of whom to form a court, who shall have a common law jurisdiction, and reside in the district, and have each therein a freehold estate in five hundred acres of land, while in the exercise of their offices; and their commissions shall continue in force during good behaviour.

The governor and judges, or a majority of them, shall adopt and publish in the district, such laws of the original states, criminal and civil, as may be necessary, and best suited to the circumstances of the district, and report them to Congress, from time to time, which laws shall be in force in the district until the organization of the general assembly therein, unless disapproved of by Congress; but afterwards the legislature shall have authority to alter them as they shall think fit.

The governor for the time being, shall be commander in chief of the militia, appoint and commission all officers in the same, below the rank of general officers; all general officers shall be appointed and commissioned by Congress.

Previous to the organization of the general assembly, the governor shall appoint such magistrates and other civil officers, in each county or township, as he shall find necessary for the preservation of the peace and good order in the same: After the general assembly shall be organized, the powers and duties of magistrates and other civil officers shall be regulated and defined by the said assembly; but all magistrates and other civil officers, not herein otherwise directed, shall, during the continuance of this temporary government, be appointed by the governor.

For the prevention of crimes and injuries, the laws to be adopted or made shall have force in all parts of the district, and for the execution of process, criminal and civil, the governor shall make proper divisions thereof—and he shall proceed from time to time, as circumstances may require, to lay out the parts of the district in which the Indian titles shall have been extinguished, into counties and townships, subject, however, to such alterations as may thereafter be made by the legislature.

So soon as there shall be five thousand free male inhabitants, of full age, in the district, upon giving proof thereof to the governor, they shall receive authority, with time and place, to elect representatives from their counties or townships, to represent them in the general assembly; provided that for every five hundred free male inhabitants there shall be one representative, and so on progressively with the number of free male inhabitants, shall the right of representation increase, until the number of representatives shall amount to twenty-five, after which the number and proportion of representatives shall be regulated by the legislature; provided that no person be eligible or qualified to act as a representative, unless he shall have been a citizen of one of the United States three years and be a resident in the district, or unless he shall have resided in the district three years, and in either case shall likewise hold in his own right, in fee simple, two hundred acres of land within the same:—Provided also, that a freehold in fifty acres of land in the district, having been a citizen of one of the states, and being resident in the district; or the like freehold and two years residence in the district shall be necessary to qualify a man as an elector of a representative.

The representatives thus elected, shall serve for the term of two years, and in case of the death of a representative, or removal from office, the governor shall issue a writ to the county or township for which he was a member, to elect another in his stead, to serve for the residue of the term.

The general assembly, or legislature, shall consist of the governor, legislative council, and a house of representatives. The legislative council shall consist of five members, to continue in office five years, unless sooner removed by Congress, any three of whom to be a quorum, and the members of the council shall be nominated and appointed in the following manner, to wit: As soon as representatives shall be elected, the governor shall appoint a time and place for them to meet together, and, when met, they shall nominate ten persons, residents in the district, and each possessed of a freehold in five hundred acres of land, and return their names to Congress; five of whom Congress shall appoint and commission to serve as aforesaid; and whenever a vacancy shall happen in the council, by death or removal from office, the house of representatives shall nominate two persons, qualified as aforesaid, for each vacancy, and return their names to Congress; one of whom Congress shall appoint and commission for the residue of the term; and every five years, four months at least before the expiration of the time of service of the members of council, the said house shall nominate ten persons, qualified as aforesaid, and return their names to Congress, five of whom Congress shall appoint and commission to serve as members of the council five years, unless sooner removed. And the governor, legislative council, and house of re-

The Importance of the Northwest Ordinance

by Peter S. Onuf

The Northwest Ordinance is one of the most important documents in American history. Approved by the Old Continental Congress, then sitting in New York, on July 13, 1787, the Ordinance provided for the creation of new states and the orderly expansion of the union. The commitment to continental development embodied in the Ordinance was as crucial to the new nation's future as the nearly simultaneous decision to institute a more "energetic" national government.

The Constitutional Convention deliberated in Philadelphia at the same time Congress, meeting in New York, fashioned its new western policy. The connection between the new federal Constitution and the Northwest Ordinance is more than chronological: it was apparent to most contemporaries that the government of the United States would have to be much stronger than it was to implement Congress's western policy. Thus the drafters of the Ordinance proceeded in the faith that the convention would succeed in its task, notwithstanding dire predictions about the Union's early demise and the subsequent formation of distinct and hostile regional confederacies.

Just as the framers proceeded without a clear constitutional mandate, Congress may have exceeded its authority under the Articles of Confederation when it promised to admit new states. The Philadelphia Convention remedied this defect by empowering Congress to administer

7

national territory and admit new states in Article IV, Section III of the new Constitution. Misgivings about the status of the Constitution itself would be laid to rest by popular ratification.

The Northwest Ordinance and the federal Constitution depended on each other. Without the Constitution, the Ordinance probably would have been a dead letter. The reverse is also probably true: the success of the new constitutional order depended on the Ordinance's commitment to a dynamic, expanding Union of equal states. The Constitution did not require expansion; it only enabled the new federal government to fulfill promises made by the Confederation Congress in the Northwest Ordinance.

The Problem of Union

In the 1780's the Union appeared on the verge of collapse. The future of the West seemed particularly problematic—and Congress had to do something about it immediately. A "bountiful providence" had favored the new nation with rich natural endowments promising boundless prosperity and power. But rapid, unregulated settlement jeopardized this promise by provoking Indians to fight for their lands while depriving Congress of desperately needed revenue from land sales. The exodus of productive citizens (and taxpayers) also threatened the old states with depopulation and poverty. Meanwhile, unauthorized settlers defied state and national authority in hopes of holding onto these lands; they set up illegal new states and warned easterners that if their pretensions were not duly recognized, they would break away from the Union and even seek alliances with neighboring imperial powers. Commentators feared that disunion—the failure to connect new settlements to old—would lead inexorably to the renewal of war, with American independence ultimately lost to the forces of counterrevolution.

The "critical period" described so vividly in Federalist rhetoric during the controversy over the ratification of the Constitution was in many ways anticipated by the crisis in the West. In its basic form, the problem facing western policy-makers between 1784 and 1787 was one of Union. Did or could easterners and westerners have interests in common that could hold them in Union? What political structures could accommodate the addition of new states? Was it possible to reconcile individual liberty and republican forms of government with an "energetic" national regime capable of maintaining law and order and holding its own against powerful enemies? These were the same questions, all variations on the problem of the "extended republic," that the framers subsequently confronted at the Philadelphia Convention.

The two central statements of congressional western policy, the Land Ordinance of May 20, 1785, and the Northwest Ordinance, represented positive answers to pervasive doubts about the future of the Union. Congress indicated its faith in the Union's survival—and helped secure it—by establishing a framework for western economic and political development. At a time when northerners and southerners, shippers and planters, small states and large states were all questioning each other's good faith, Congress affirmed the nation's commitment to the vast project of continental development.

What sort of Union did Congress contemplate? The central premise of congressional western policy was set forth in September and October 1780 when the large, "landed" states were called on to relinquish their extensive western claims to make possible the creation of a national domain. Congress then promised, and the promise was repeated in state land cessions, that land sales revenue would be used for the "common benefit" of the United States and that western settlements eventually would be formed into new, equal states and be admitted into the Union. The Union, therefore, would not simply be a confederation of fully sovereign states dedicated to the preservation and extension of their territorial pretensions. But neither would it become a consolidated, continental republic: the expansion of the United States was made synonymous with the creation of new states. In this way Congress was able to avoid the fundamental flaw of British imperial policy. Unlike the original thirteen states which had had to break from the empire in order to assert their equality, the new American "colonies" in the West could look forward to being received as equal members of the Union.

Once Virginia had ceded its trans-Ohio claims (in March 1784) and Congress finally had a domain to administer, a committee headed by Thomas Jefferson quickly developed procedures for forming new states. The territorial government ordinance of April 23, 1784, the direct predecessor of the Northwest Ordinance, reaffirmed Congress's commitment to new state equality. In the movement toward national constitutional reform, nationalists like James Madison and Alexander Hamilton spoke disparagingly of the states; if they could not be abolished, they should at least be clearly subordinate to the central government. But there was no question for congressional policy-makers, whatever their own preferences, that the promise of statehood was the *sine qua non* of expansion. They grasped in a practical way the political realities that later made nationalists into "federalists" who promised that the new regime would preserve and strengthen—and not destroy—the states.

Yet congressmen had no illusions about the dangers of democratic excesses on the local and state level. Conservative easterners had always been skeptical about the political character and virtue of frontierspeople who, they thought, sought to escape the restraints of taxation, law, and civilized society by moving west. Given these preconceptions, how could congressmen ever hope to incorporate these licentious "white savages" into the American Union? Fear of popular power led conservative nationalists to seek curbs on state sovereignty. But for western policy-makers, the solution was to delay the onset of self-government and statehood during a period of political apprenticeship under appointed territorial officials.

The new "colonial" policy set forth in the Northwest Ordinance was premised on the analogy of political development to individual growth from childhood to maturity. Congressmen thus were able to reconcile their "realistic" assessment of the settlers' capacity—or lack of capacity—for self-government with an ultimate commitment to republican principles. Setting the population threshold for independent statehood at 60,000 (the population of Delaware) also allayed anxieties of the original states about being outvoted in Congress by small, poor, underdeveloped new states: the new states would become more or less equal in fact—at least compared to the smaller old states—before they could claim an equal standing in the Union. Congressional western policy further countered the centrifugal effects of expansion by establishing territorial governments that could guarantee federal property interests during the crucial first years of settlement.

Because congressmen assumed the worst about westerners, they designed a framework for territorial development that would gradually prepare them for political responsibility. The land ordinance therefore provided material support for local education and Article III of the Northwest Ordinance proclaimed that "schools and the means of education shall forever be encouraged." But Congress's western policy was also "educational" in a much broader sense. Controlled settlement (or what George Washington called "progressive seating") under the land ordinance would prevent the reversion to savagery that scattered settlement supposedly entailed. The relatively high price of lands would screen out impecunious, antisocial, subsistence-oriented squatters; sober, industrious, commercial farmers would be attracted by the promise of orderly conditions, secure titles, and ready access to markets. The grid pattern of land surveys would eliminate the divisive title conflicts that retarded settlement and subverted communal harmony in Kentucky and other frontier areas. Clustered settlements would be more easily defended against external enemies and internal disorder and the rapid development of churches, schools, courts, and other local institutions would facilitate the passage to self-government. Assuming this process of social development, the authors of the Northwest Ordinance provided for the gradual substitution of home rule for government by appointed officials.

Jefferson's 1784 ordinance focused on the attainment of statehood, neglecting the earlier political development of the frontier settlements. Ironically, as subsequent congressional committees recognized, a permissive regime that left settlers to their own devices was bound to attract the kinds of settlers *least* able (by eastern standards) to govern themselves and most likely to provoke the Indians and engage in political and diplomatic intrigues. If the new states then gained early admission to the Union, they would doubtless use their power to vindicate dubious land titles and wrest public lands from a weak federal government. According to this logic, settlers *most* capable of governing themselves would be unwilling to venture west unless Congress could guarantee law, order, and property rights. As promoters of the Ohio Company purchase made clear, industrious New Englanders demanded that an effective colonial government be present at the very beginning of settlement. Only when their new communities were firmly established would it be possible to recreate the political life they had left behind.

But the extension of republican government, policy-makers knew, was not

10

itself a sufficient guarantee of continuing union. They recognized that only the development of common interests could bind easterners and westerners to a common destiny. During the debate over the new Constitution, the existence—or nonexistence—of such interests was a much-disputed point: it logically preceded the still more controversial question of whether or not republican liberty could survive under a more vigorous continental government. But the authors of congressional western policy insisted that the interests of different sections could be harmonized under certain conditions: the clustering of new settlements near old ones would not only facilitate political control but would help foster economic ties; improved transportation—roads, canals, and river improvements—would bring East and West closer together.

Washington, Jefferson and other advocates of internal improvements grasped the political as well as economic implications of opening up the western trade. Without an "easy communication," wrote Washington, the westerners "will become a distinct people from us." Recognizing that mutually beneficial trade was the only durable bond of union, congressmen hoped to encourage westerners to cultivate strong ties to the east; for their part, easterners could look for prosperous returns from new western markets. A new conception of the Union, premised less on political affinities than on free exchange and complementary interest, was implicit in western policy. It was the same conception that Federalists invoked in making their case for a stronger central government.

The Northwest Ordinance not only affirmed Congress's faith in the Union, but also included specific measures for assuring its survival and expansion. Looking west and glimpsing the possibility that controlled political and economic development could make westerners into good republicans while directing their enterprise into channels beneficial to the whole Union, easterners might also imagine transcending the debilitating conflicts among interest groups, sections, and states that had immobilized the Confederation. Without such a vision, Antifederalist warnings about the dangers of "despotism" and "consolidation" would have been unanswerable. What was the point of union if it did not serve the real interests of all parts of the continent?

The Ordinance and the Constitution

The Northwest Ordinance was an integral part of America's new constitutional order. Provisions for western expansion gave substance to the national idea, offering a plausible model for continental economic development and intersectional harmony. In the context of the 1780s, it is clear that the Ordinance and the Constitution depended on—and even completed—each other. But, in retrospect, the reputation of the Ordinance has been eclipsed. There are several related reasons for this.

Union was the preeminent problem of the 1780s. Providing a mechanism for securing and extending the union—and guaranteeing that the United States rather than Great Britain, Spain, or a new western confederacy would be able to develop the fertile hinterland—was crucial. But the Ordinance's very success made western policy seem less centrally important to national history: once Congress's authority in the territories was well-established and unruly settlers presented a less serious threat to national security, expansion became more routine and union less problematic—until, of course, the sectional crisis tore it apart.

The authority of the Constitution has been progressively extended through amendments and judicial interpretations. In contrast, because much of the Ordinance was designed to become obsolete, its authority diminished over time: as a "living" constitutional text it contracted rather than expanded. The first section of the Ordinance, establishing a system of temporary territorial administration, became inoperative with the attainment of statehood. Congress always considered these provisions subject to change, beginning in 1789 when it reenacted the Ordinance in slightly altered form to make the territorial system compatible with the new federal regime. By the time Congress passed the organic law for Wisconsin Territory in 1836 the Ordinance's government provisions were almost entirely superseded.

Even the supposedly permanent compact articles that completed the Ordinance tended to become obsolete. Guarantees of civil liberties and property rights (Article II) were applicable in the territorial period; they could—and did—take on different form when Northwesterners drafted their own constitutions. Other broad injunctions were either unexceptionable (namely the provision for freedom of worship in Article I) or unenforceable (the promise of "justice and humanity" towards the Indians in Article III). The articles governing state constitution-writing, defining boundaries, and providing for admission to the Union (IV and V) did have permanent effects, but they also ceased to operate once the statehood process was complete.

Only two provisions of the Ordinance continued to be relevant to the constitutional history of the Northwestern states after they were admitted to the Union. The stipulation in Article IV that the "waters leading into the Mississippi and Saint Lawrence" remain "common highways" was invoked as a constitutional bar to various obstructions to free navigation. Article VI, prohibiting the introduction of slavery, was much more controversial. Although free soil Northwesterners rebuffed attempts to legalize slavery (most notably in Indiana in 1802-03 and in Illinois in 1823-24), debate on the relative advantages and disadvantages of the institution tended to undercut the binding authority of Article VI. The Northwest remained free because that was the will of its people, not because of Congress's decree.

The last word on the constitutional standing of the Northwest Ordinance came from Chief Justice Roger Taney in *Strader* v. *Graham* (1850). Taney asserted that the Ordinance was a constitutional nullity. The compact articles "were said to be perpetual," but they had *not* been incorporated in the federal Constitution: "they certainly are not superior and paramount to the Constitution." In Taney's estimation, at least, the text of the Ordinance no longer had any authority at all: it had virtually disappeared. While the courts subsequently backed off from this extreme position in various free commerce cases, Taney's opinion accurately reflected the prevalent understanding of the relationship between the Ordinance and the Constitution.

Regional Symbol

The "defects" of the Northwest Ordinance as a constitutional text were illuminated by its changing relation to the federal Constitution. The ascendancy of the Constitution in the popular imagination diminished the Ordinance's lustre: the cult of the founding fathers left other revolutionary statesmen in the shadows. The elevation of the founders was premised on an invidious comparison with those second-rate politicians who served the old and "imbecilic" Congress in its waning days. Thus, Taney and other critics of the Ordinance suggested, the Continental Congress had no authority to bind its successors; it certainly could not preempt and control the will of the sovereign people expressed through its delegates in Philadelphia.

The form of the Ordinance constituted another telling deficiency. When Congress acted, it was by no means clear what an authoritative constitutional text should look like. As "owner" of the western lands, the United States acting through Congress exercised the unquestionable authority of a "sovereign" in establishing the terms on which land could be purchased, while guaranteeing law and order and promising to extend political privileges. This was precisely the form taken by colonial charters: what other provision could be made for (supposedly) unsettled territory? But in the light of emerging constitutional standards, the authority exercised by Congress through its officials increasingly came to be seen as arbitrary and despotic. Many impatient settlers thus began to turn against the Ordinance as a symbol of their colonial degradation.

As the constitutional authority of the Ordinance came increasingly under attack, the checkered history of its composition became apparent. When later generations of Northwesterners looked back on their early history they were hard-pressed to identify the document's actual authors. In contrast to the "founders" at Philadelphia, the members of successive congressional committees who helped formulate territorial policy gave little thought to their immortal reputations. The final text was hurriedly drafted under the press of events; the slavery prohibition in Article VI was tacked on at the last minute. The integrity of the Ordinance's text was further compromised by subsequent controversy and revision. Even commentators who celebrated specific provisions often did so at the expense of the rest of the document. Proponents of statehood in Ohio, for instance, relied on the compact promises to liberate them from "colonial" subjection while condemning the "despotic" territorial government authorized in the first part of the

Ordinance. And by the 1830s the slavery prohibition seemed so centrally important that the rest of the Ordinance was virtually neglected.

Yet even as the Northwest Ordinance was picked apart and its various provisions were revised, discarded, or ignored, the document emerged as a powerful symbol of regional identity. The Ordinance, Ohioan Caleb Atwater wrote, was "justly considered as the Magna Carta of Ohio, and all of the states northwest of the Ohio river." Northwesterners celebrated the Ordinance by emphasizing its central role in the founding of their states and identifying its authors with the founders of the republic. They focused on what Salmon Chase called "the genuine principles of freedom" supposedly underlying the text, not on its specific language. One patriotic orator suggested that "the principles of the Revolution mingled with (the region's) very soil by the ordinance of '87." Another eulogist asserted that "that blessed boon sprang from the profound regard of the Fathers of the Republic for the Rights of Man."

The developing sectional crisis focused new attention on the Ordinance as a charter of freedom. Because of the Northwest Ordinance and its companion land ordinance "we have had flowing towards us, a flood of immigrants who love liberty"; "those excellent laws of Congress" furnished "a perfect mould for well proportioned republicans." By the 1820s a vast migration from the free states had already tipped the balance decisively against efforts to circumvent Article VI. Increasingly, patriotic writers attributed the region's rapid growth and sudden prosperity to the exclusion of slavery. Arguing that the founders' commitment to freedom only found full expression in the Ordinance—they had been forced to compromise with slavery in the Constitution—Northwesterners turned unfavorable comparisons between the two documents on their head. Chase thought the Ordinance "fit consummation" of the "glorious labors" of the old Congress, "unadulterated by that compromise with circumstances" that marred other great state papers, "the effects of which are visible in the constitution and history of the union."

The apotheosis of the Northwest Ordinance in the decades before the Civil War is replete with irony. In one sense, celebrations of the document reflected the declining authority and increasing irrelevance of its actual text: Northwesterners could rally round the Ordinance because it was no longer controversial. And, paradoxically, a document that had helped make *union* a substantial reality in the 1780s was now invoked to illuminate the fundamental differences between free states and slave states and thus ultimately to rationalize *disunion.*

It is also ironic that the reputation of the Ordinance has been compromised despite—and perhaps even because of—its crucial role in the early history of the republic. For subsequent generations, union, the great desideratum of the founding era, seemed inevitable and the mid-nineteenth century crisis of the union a tragic, inexplicable exception in the course of American political development. As a key to establishing a durable Union, the Ordinance is naturally overshadowed by the Constitution; as a symbol of sectional distinctiveness in the antebellum decades, it has been overlooked by subsequent generations of Americans in their eagerness to reaffirm national union.

Our high regard for the federal Constitution, a "living" text that continues to shape American life, has never required—however much it would benefit from—an accurate understanding of its historical context. But a proper appreciation of the Northwest Ordinance does depend on our historical sense; only by reconstructing the challenges facing earlier generations can we assess the impact of this neglected document on regional and national history.

Peter S. Onuf has recently been named professor of history at Southern Methodist University. Educated at Johns Hopkins University where he received his Ph.D. in 1973, Professor Onuf has taught at the University of California at San Diego, Columbia University, and in the Humanities Department at Worcester Polytechnic Intitute, 1980-1987. He has been awarded major grants from the National Endowment for the Humanities and Project '87 and is the author of numerous works on early American political and contitutional history. His *Statehood and Union: A History of the Northwest Ordinance* is being published this year by Indiana University Press.

Recommended reading: Most of the themes of this essay are further developed in Peter S. Onuf, *Statehood and Union: A History of the Northwest Ordinance* (Bloomington, 1987). The best discussion of political thought in the founding period is in Gordon S. Wood, *The Creation of the American Republic, 1776-1787* (Chapel Hill, 1969); the history of the old Congress is recounted in Jack N. Rakove, *The Beginnings of National Politics: An Interpretive History of the Continental Congress* (New York, 1979). Robert Berkhofer, Jr., "Jefferson, the Ordinance of 1784, and the Origins of the American Territorial System," *William and Mary Quarterly*, 3rd ser., 29 (1972), 231-62, provides valuable insight into the evolution of territorial policy. On political economy see Drew McCoy, *The Elusive Republic: Political Economy in Jeffersonian America* (Chapel Hill, 1980); Joyce Appleby, *Capitalism and a New Social Order: The Republican Vision of the 1790s* (New York, 1984); Forrest McDonald, *Novus Ordo Seclorum: The Intellectual Origins of the Constitution* (Lawrence, Kans., 1985), 97-142; and Cathy Matson and Peter Onuf, "Toward a Republican Empire: Interest and Ideology in Revolutionary America," *American Quarterly* 37 (1985), 496-531. For a good recent treatment of early Ohio history see Andrew R. L. Cayton, *The Frontier Republic: Ideology and Politics in the Ohio Country, 1780-1825* (Kent, Ohio, 1986). Don Fehrenbacher's *The Dred Scott Case: Its Significance in American Law and Politics* (New York, 1978), includes a fine discussion of the problem of slavery in the territories. For analysis of the meaning of "freedom" in free soil rhetoric see Eric Foner, *Free Soil, Free Labor, Free Men: The Ideology of the Republican Party before the Civil War* (New York, 1970). The historiography of the Ordinance is reviewed in Philip R. Shriver, "America's Other Bicentennial," *The Old Northwest* 9 (1983), 219-35.

The Northwest Ordinance

It is sometimes said that the basic documents for the founding of the United States are the Declaration of Independence, 1776, the Ordinance of 1787, and the Constitution, 1787-8. The two hundredth anniversary of the first was observed more than a decade ago; the bicentennial of the latter two is currently being celebrated. This traveling exhibition represents a joint effort by universities, historical societies, and libraries in the six states formed out of the Old Northwest.

To encourage settlement in the Northwest Territory, the Congress of the Confederation had in place an ordinance embodying a system of reliable measurement of lands to be sold so that indisputable titles could be issued. But that was not enough. The second need was for some plan of government clearly set forth in stages from ruling officials appointed by Congress to elected state governments joining the Union. This original idea was set forth and explained in the Ordinance of 1787.

The books, manuscripts, maps, and prints selected to illustrate the life of the Ordinance begin with a growing consciousness of our first West, the rejection of colonialism, the guarantee of individual rights, the problems of Indian treaties and the issues that led to the War of 1812, the challenge of self-determination, and ultimate inclusion in the Union of states on a footing of equality. If there seems to be a breathlessness in this development, it probably reflects the constant changes in growing responsibilities. It is an instructive story of a stable but flexible charter that allowed thirty-one of our fifty states to be carved out of the public domain under the Ordinance of 1787 as amended from time to time. With the admission of Minnesota as a state, the application of the Ordinance to the Old Northwest came to an end but the pattern remained in force.

Intransigent Spain and Portugal lost their American colonies by revolt. As for France, Napoleon sold us Louisiana so that he could devote his resources to a futile effort to conquer Europe. Russia sold us Alaska. Great Britain, a slow learner, eventually conferred dominion status on Canada and its other colonies until the empire was only a sentimental connection of self-governing members. Germany came late on the empire scene and its only colonies (in Africa and the Pacific) were lost in World War I. The genius of the Ordinance of 1787 remained unique.

John C. Dann
Director, Clements Library
The University of Michigan

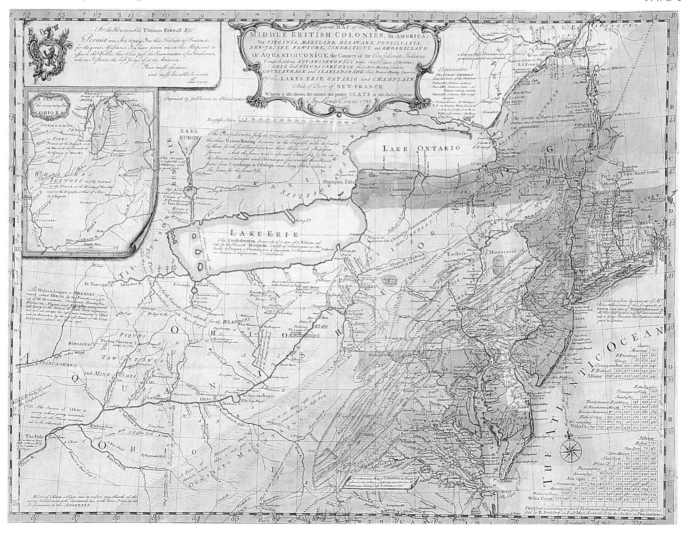

NWO-3

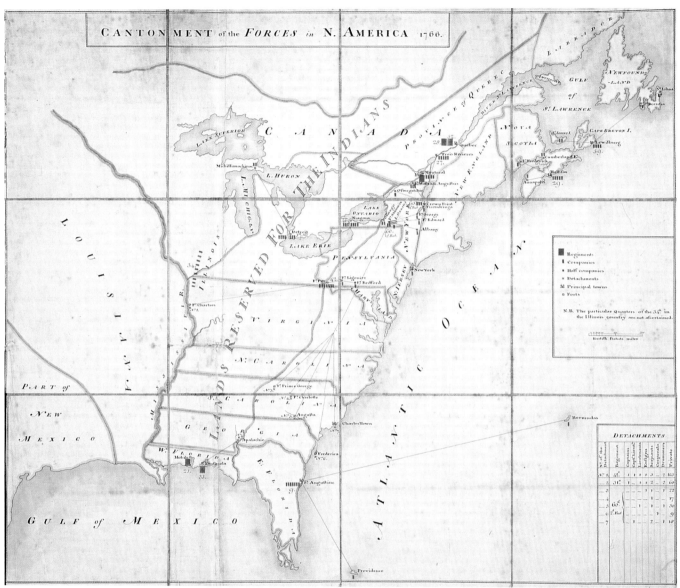

NWO-6

19

NWO-14

NWO-1.
Lewis Evans, *A General Map of the Middle British colonies in America: of Aquanishounigy, the country of the Confederate Indians;. . . of the Lakes Erie, Ontario and Champlain, and Part of New France. . .* Philadelphia, 1755. Colored map, 20 x 27 1/4.

See illustration on page 17

Lilly Library

This map was the first to make the coastal colonies aware of the inland area west of the Allegheny Mountains—what became known as the Ohio country or the Northwest. It was accompanied by a thirty-two page pamphlet entitled *Geographical, Historical, Political, Philosophical and Mechanical Essays,* in which Evans emphasized the advantages to the British colonies of controlling the Ohio country. He was sure the French were exceeding their rightful boundary in Canada and pushing their way southward to the Ohio River. Indeed, the French and Indian War had started by the time his map and *Essays* reached print. His detached map was widely pirated and was the prototype for other map makers for many years.

NWO-2.
[Benjamin Franklin,] *The Interest of Great Britain with regard to her Colonies, and the Acquisitions of Canada and Guadaloupe. . .* London: Printed for T. Becket. MDCCLX. 58 p.

Lilly Library

After the fall of Quebec in 1759 and then the capture of Guadaloupe, vigorous debate arose in Parliament whether to keep or turn back one of these conquests as part of the peace negotiations. Some Englishmen regarded the sugar producing island in the Caribbean as more valuable. Franklin, writing anonymously, as if he were an Englishman, argued that both for security and economic reasons Canada should be retained. The pamphlet went through five editions that year, so it must have been widely read in England and America. Its point of view prevailed.

NWO-3.
Benjamin West, *The Death of General Wolfe,* engraved by Augustin LeGrand, Paris, 1776. Colored print, 20 x 24.

See illustration on page 18

Clements Library

The climax of the French and Indian War was the capture of Quebec in September 1759 by the British. The commanders on both sides were killed. The fall of Montreal in 1760 resulted in the surrender of Canada to the British.

West, an American artist active in London, produced a large oil painting of the death of Wolfe, exhibited in 1771. He did four originals; one hangs in the Clements Library. The picture had strong patriotic appeal and captured the public imagination; hence engravings were extremely popular.

NWO-4.
Preliminary Articles of Peace between His Britannick Majesty. . . and the Catholick King signed at Fontainebleau, the 3d day of November, 1762. London: Printed by E. Owen and T. Harrison. 1762. 23 p.

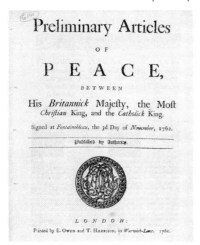

This preliminary peace treaty of 1762 and the final treaty signed February 10, 1763, differed only in minor details. In North America, France ceded to Great Britain, Canada and all its dependencies and several West Indian Islands. That part of Louisiana lying west of the Mississippi River was given by France to Spain in compensation for Florida, which Spain yielded to Great Britain. France was thus expelled from North America.

In debating the *Preliminary Articles* in Parliament, Lord Shelburne pointed out the benefits to the English colonies in America, "now freed from the molestations of enemies and the emulation of rivals, unlimited in their possessions, and safe in their persons." Indeed, they were free to concentrate on their complaints against British rule for the next dozen years.

NWO-5.
By the King, A Proclamation. . . London: Printed by Mark Baskett. 1763. Broadside, 24 x 18.

Pontiac's Indian uprising at Detroit in 1763 emphasized one trouble Great Britain would face in its new western territory: settlement by whites on Indian land. To preserve peace along the frontier, Britain attempted to prevent settlement beyond the crest of the Appalachian Mountains by this Proclamation of October 1763. Unfortunately, would-be settlers paid little attention to the Proclamation or to protests of the resident Indian tribes. The Indians continued to complain and threaten and to build up resentment.

NWO-6.
"Cantonment of the Forces in N. America 1766." Manuscript map, 22 x 24

See illustration on page 19

In spite of Indian treaties and efforts to prevent English settlements, former French forts in the new West had to be garrisoned by British regulars to discourage frontier raids. In other words, the acquisition of Canada in 1763 cost Great Britain heavily to maintain. The mainland colonies resented having to pay through taxes for this dubious protection. The map illustrates how the London government saw the area in military terms.

By the KING,

A PROCLAMATION.

GEORGE R.

WHEREAS We have taken into Our Royal Conſideration the extenſive and valuable Acquiſitions in *America*, ſecured to Our Crown by the late Definitive Treaty of Peace, concluded at *Paris* the Tenth Day of *February* laſt; and being deſirous, that all Our loving Subjects, as well of Our Kingdoms as of Our Colonies in *America*, may avail themſelves, with all convenient Speed, of the great Benefits and Advantages which muſt accrue therefrom to their Commerce, Manufactures, and Navigation; We have thought fit, with the Advice of Our Privy Council, to iſſue this Our Royal Proclamation, hereby to publiſh and declare to all Our loving Subjects, that We have, with the Advice of Our ſaid Privy Council, granted Our Letters Patent under Our Great Seal of *Great Britain*, to erect within the Countries and Iſlands ceded and confirmed to Us by the ſaid Treaty, Four diſtinct and ſeparate Governments, ſtiled and called by the Names of *Quebec*, *Eaſt Florida*, *Weſt Florida*, and *Grenada*, and limited and bounded as follows; *viz.*

Firſt. The Government of *Quebec*, bounded on the *Labrador* Coaſt by the River *St. John*, and from thence by a Line drawn from the Head of that River through the Lake *St. John* to the South End of the Lake nigh *Piſſin*; from whence the ſaid Line croſſing the River *St. Lawrence* and the Lake *Champlain* in Forty five Degrees of North Latitude, paſſes along the High Lands which divide the Rivers that empty themſelves into the ſaid River *St. Lawrence*, from thoſe which fall into the Sea; and alſo along the North Coaſt of the *Baye des Chaleurs*, and the Coaſt of the Gulph of *St. Lawrence* to Cape *Roſieres*, and from thence croſſing the Mouth of the River *St. Lawrence* by the Weſt End of the Iſland of *Anticoſti*, terminates at the aforeſaid River of *St. John*.

Secondly. The Government of *Eaſt Florida*, bounded to the Weſtward by the Gulph of *Mexico*, and the *Apalachicola* River; to the Northward, by a Line drawn from that Part of the ſaid River where the *Chatahouchee* and *Flint* Rivers meet, to the Source of *St. Mary's* River, and by the Courſe of the ſaid River to the *Atlantick* Ocean; and to the Eaſtward and Southward, by the *Atlantick* Ocean, and the Gulph of *Florida*, including all Iſlands within Six Leagues of the Sea Coaſt.

Thirdly. The Government of *Weſt Florida*, bounded to the Southward by the Gulph of *Mexico*, including all Iſlands within Six Leagues of the Coaſt from the River *Apalachicola* to Lake *Pontchartrain*; to the Weſtward by that Part of the River *Miſſiſippi* which lies in Thirty one Degrees [illegible] the Northward, by a Line drawn due Eaſt from [illegible] *Apalachicola* or *Chatahouchee*; and to the Eaſtward by the ſaid River.

Fourthly. The Government of *Grenada*, comprehending the Iſland of that Name, together with the *Grenadines*, and the Iſlands of *Dominico*, *St. Vincents*, and *Tobago*.

And, to the End that the open and free Fiſhery of Our Subjects may be extended to and carried on upon the Coaſt of *Labrador* and the adjacent Iſlands, We have thought fit, with the Advice of Our ſaid Privy Council, to put all that Coaſt, from the River *St. John's* to *Hudſon's Streights*, together with the Iſlands of *Anticoſti* and *Madelaine*, and all other ſmaller Iſlands lying upon the ſaid Coaſt, under the Care and Inſpection of Our Governor of *Newfoundland*.

We have alſo, with the Advice of Our Privy Council, thought fit to annex the Iſlands of *St. John's*, and *Cape Breton* or *Iſle Royale*, with the leſſer Iſlands adjacent thereto, to Our Government of *Nova Scotia*.

We have alſo, with the Advice of Our Privy Council aforeſaid, annexed to Our Province of *Georgia* all the Lands lying between the Rivers *Attamaha* and *St. Mary's*.

And whereas it will greatly contribute to the ſpeedy ſettling Our ſaid new Governments, that Our loving Subjects ſhould be informed of Our Paternal Care for the Security of the Liberties and Properties of thoſe who are and ſhall become Inhabitants thereof; We have thought fit to publiſh and declare, by this Our Proclamation, that We have, in the Letters Patent under Our Great Seal of *Great Britain*, by which the ſaid Governments are conſtituted, given expreſs Power and Direction to Our Governors of Our ſaid Colonies reſpectively, that ſo ſoon as the State and Circumſtances of the ſaid Colonies will admit thereof, they ſhall, with the Advice and Conſent of the Members of Our Council, ſummon and call General Aſſemblies within the ſaid Governments reſpectively, in ſuch Manner and Form as is uſed and directed in thoſe Colonies and Provinces in *America*, which are under Our immediate Government; and We have alſo given Power to the ſaid Governors, with the Conſent of Our ſaid Councils, and the Repreſentatives of the People, ſo to be ſummoned as aforeſaid, to make, conſtitute, and ordain Laws, Statutes, and Ordinances for the Publick Peace, Welfare, and Good Government of Our ſaid Colonies, and of the People and Inhabitants thereof, as near as may be agreeable to the Laws of *England*, and under ſuch Regulations and Reſtrictions as are uſed in other Colonies: And in the mean Time, and until ſuch Aſſemblies can be called as aforeſaid, all Perſons inhabiting in, or reſorting to Our ſaid Colonies, may confide in Our Royal Protection for the Enjoyment of the Benefit of the Laws of Our Realm of *England*; for which Purpoſe, We have given Power under Our Great Seal to the Governors of Our ſaid Colonies reſpectively, to erect and conſtitute, with the Advice of Our ſaid Councils reſpectively, Courts of Judicature and Publick Juſtice, within Our ſaid Colonies, for the hearing and determining all Cauſes, as well Criminal as Civil, according to Law and Equity, and as near as may be agreeable to the Laws of *England*, with Liberty to all Perſons who may think themſelves aggrieved by the Sentences of ſuch Courts, in all Civil Caſes, to appeal, under the uſual Limitations and Reſtrictions, to Us in Our Privy Council.

We have alſo thought fit, with the Advice of Our Privy Council as aforeſaid, to give unto the Governors and Councils of Our ſaid Three New Colonies upon the Continent, full Power and Authority to ſettle and agree with the Inhabitants of Our ſaid New Colonies, or with any other Perſons who ſhall reſort thereto, for ſuch Lands, Tenements, and Hereditaments, as are now, or hereafter ſhall be in Our Power to diſpoſe of, and them to grant to any ſuch Perſon or Perſons, upon ſuch Terms, and under ſuch moderate Quit-Rents, Services, and Acknowledgements as have been appointed and ſettled in Our other Colonies, and under ſuch other Conditions as ſhall appear to Us to be neceſſary and expedient for the Advantage of the Grantees, and the Improvement and Settlement of Our ſaid Colonies.

And whereas We are deſirous, upon all Occaſions, to teſtify Our Royal Senſe and Approbation of the Conduct and Bravery of the Officers and Soldiers of Our Armies, and to reward the ſame, We do hereby command and impower Our Governors of Our ſaid Three New Colonies, and all other Our Governors of Our ſeveral Provinces on the Continent of *North America*, to grant, without Fee or Reward, to ſuch Reduced Officers as have ſerved in *North America* during the late War, and to ſuch Private Soldiers as have been or ſhall be diſbanded in *America*, and are actually reſiding there, and ſhall perſonally apply for the ſame, the following Quantities of Lands, ſubject at the Expiration of Ten Years to the ſame Quit-Rents as other Lands are ſubject to in the Province within which they are granted, as alſo ſubject to the ſame Conditions of Cultivation and Improvement; *viz.*

To every Perſon having the Rank of a Field Officer, Five thouſand Acres.—To every Captain, Three thouſand Acres.—To every Subaltern or Staff Officer, Two thouſand Acres.—To every Non-Commiſſion Officer, Two hundred Acres.—To every Private Man, Fifty Acres.

We do likewiſe authorize and require the Governors and Commanders in Chief of all Our ſaid Colonies upon the Continent of *North America*, to grant the like Quantities of Land, and upon the ſame Conditions, to ſuch Reduced Officers of Our Navy, of like Rank, as ſerved on Board Our Ships of War in *North America* at the Times of the Reduction of *Louiſbourg* and *Quebec* in the late War, and who ſhall perſonally apply to Our reſpective Governors for ſuch Grants.

And whereas it is juſt and reaſonable, and eſſential to Our Intereſt and the Security of Our Colonies, that the ſeveral Nations or Tribes of *Indians*, with whom We are connected, and who live under Our Protection, ſhould not be moleſted or diſturbed in the Poſſeſſion of ſuch Parts of Our Dominions and Territories as, not having been ceded to, or purchaſed by Us, are reſerved to them, or any of them, as their Hunting Grounds; We do therefore, with the Advice of Our Privy Council, declare it to be Our Royal Will and Pleaſure, that no Governor or Commander in Chief in any of Our Colonies of *Quebec*, *Eaſt Florida*, or *Weſt Florida*, do preſume, upon any Pretence whatever, to grant Warrants of Survey, or paſs any Patents for Lands beyond the Bounds of their reſpective Governments, as deſcribed in their Commiſſions; as alſo, that no Governor or Commander in Chief in any of Our other Colonies or Plantations in *America*, do preſume, for the preſent, and until Our further Pleaſure be known, to grant Warrants of Survey, or paſs Patents for any Lands beyond the Heads or Sources of any of the Rivers which fall into the *Atlantick* Ocean from the Weſt and North Weſt, or upon any Lands whatever, which, not having been ceded to or purchaſed by Us as aforeſaid, are reſerved to the ſaid *Indians*, or any of them.

And We do further declare it to be Our Royal Will and Pleaſure, for the preſent as aforeſaid, to reſerve under Our Sovereignty, Protection, and Dominion, for the Uſe of the ſaid *Indians*, all the Lands and Territories not included within the Limits of Our ſaid Three New Governments, or within the Limits of the Territory granted to the *Hudſon's Bay* Company, as alſo all the Lands and Territories lying to the Weſtward of the Sources of the Rivers which fall into the Sea from the Weſt and North Weſt, as aforeſaid; and We do hereby ſtrictly forbid, on Pain of Our Diſpleaſure, all Our loving Subjects from making any Purchaſes or Settlements whatever, or taking Poſſeſſion of any of the Lands above reſerved, without Our eſpecial Leave and Licence for that Purpoſe firſt obtained.

And We do further ſtrictly enjoin and require all Perſons whatever, who have either wilfully or inadvertently ſeated themſelves upon any Lands within the Countries above deſcribed, or upon any other Lands, which, not having been ceded to, or purchaſed by Us, are ſtill reſerved to the ſaid *Indians* as aforeſaid, forthwith to remove themſelves from ſuch Settlements.

And whereas great Frauds and Abuſes have been committed in the purchaſing Lands of the *Indians*, to the great Prejudice of Our Intereſts, and to the great Diſſatisfaction of the ſaid *Indians*; in order therefore to prevent ſuch Irregularities for the future, and to the End that the *Indians* may be convinced of Our Juſtice, and determined Reſolution to remove all reaſonable Cauſe of Diſcontent, We do, with the Advice of Our Privy Council, ſtrictly enjoin and require, that no private Perſon do preſume to make any Purchaſe from the ſaid *Indians* of any Lands reſerved to the ſaid *Indians*, within thoſe Parts of Our Colonies where We have thought proper to allow Settlement; but that if, at any Time, any of the ſaid *Indians* ſhould be inclined to diſpoſe of the ſaid Lands, the ſame ſhall be purchaſed only for Us, in Our Name, at ſome Publick Meeting or Aſſembly of the ſaid *Indians* to be held for that Purpoſe by the Governor or Commander in Chief of Our Colonies reſpectively, within which they ſhall lie; and in caſe they ſhall lie within the Limits of any Proprietary Government, they ſhall be purchaſed only for the Uſe and in the Name of ſuch Proprietaries, conformable to ſuch Directions and Inſtructions as We or they ſhall think proper to give for that Purpoſe: And We do, by the Advice of Our Privy Council, declare and enjoin, that the Trade with the ſaid *Indians* ſhall be free and open to all Our Subjects whatever; provided that every Perſon, who may incline to trade with the ſaid *Indians*, do take out a Licence for carrying on ſuch Trade from the Governor or Commander in Chief of any of Our Colonies reſpectively, where ſuch Perſon ſhall reſide; and alſo give Security to obſerve ſuch Regulations as We ſhall at any Time think fit, by Ourſelves or by Our Commiſſaries to be appointed for this Purpoſe, to direct and appoint for the Benefit of the ſaid Trade; and We do hereby authorize, enjoin, and require the Governors and Commanders in Chief of all Our Colonies reſpectively, as well Thoſe under Our immediate Government as Thoſe under the Government and Direction of Proprietaries, to grant ſuch Licences without Fee or Reward, taking eſpecial Care to inſert therein a Condition, that ſuch Licence ſhall be void, and the Security forfeited, in caſe the Perſon, to whom the ſame is granted, ſhall refuſe or neglect to obſerve ſuch Regulations as We ſhall think proper to preſcribe as aforeſaid.

And We do further expreſly enjoin and require all Officers whatever, as well Military as Thoſe employed in the Management and Direction of *Indian* Affairs within the Territories reſerved as aforeſaid for the Uſe of the ſaid *Indians*, to ſeize and apprehend all Perſons whatever, who, ſtanding charged with Treaſons, Miſpriſions of Treaſon, Murders, or other Felonies or Miſdemeanors, ſhall fly from Juſtice, and take Refuge in the ſaid Territory, and to ſend them under a proper Guard to the Colony where the Crime was committed of which they ſtand accuſed, in order to take their Tryal for the ſame.

Given at Our Court at *Saint James's*, the Seventh Day of *October*, One thouſand ſeven hundred and ſixty three, in the Third Year of Our Reign.

GOD ſave the KING.

LONDON:

Printed by *Mark Baskett*, Printer to the King's moſt Excellent Majeſty; and by the Aſſigns of *Robert Baskett*. 1763.

NWO-5

NWO-7.
Thomas Hutchins, "A Plan of the
River Ohio from Fort Pitt to the
Mississippi," 1766. Colored
manuscript map, 32 1/4 x 71 1/4.
Thomas Gage papers,
Clements Library

To obtain an accurate idea of the course of the Ohio River, General Thomas Gage ordered an expedition under the command of George Croghan, Deputy Superintendent of Indian Affairs, and including Captain Harry Gordon, chief engineer in North America, and Ensign Thomas Hutchins, engineer. George Morgan of Philadelphia went along with a huge supply of trade goods. The purpose was to produce a hydrographic survey of the river. With them were about one hundred Iroquois and a considerable number of Delaware and Shawnee. They left Fort Pitt on June 18, 1766, and reached the Mississippi on August 7.

The map contains extra information about tributaries, islands, dangerous channels, and the "falls" or rapids around modern Louisville. It was primarily the work of Hutchins, this copy having been drawn by William Brasier. Captain Gordon made another map of the Ohio. The expedition turned down the Mississippi River and went as far as New Orleans before returning.

NWO-8.
Joshua Elder to John Lukens,
April 15, 1769. Paxton, Pa.
Autograph letter signed, 1 p.
Duane Norman Diedrich collection,
Clements Library

In this manuscript letter from the Deputy Surveyor to the Surveyor General of Pennsylvania he provides his personal observation that "The people are going out very fast to settle. . . I suppose I met above two hundred Men, between Ligonier and Carlisle with Horses & Utensils necessary for Building & Improving..." This evidence of the continuing pressure on the part of colonists to open the western territory to settlement was a portent of trouble to come from "squatters."

NWO-9.
*Articles of Confederation and
Perpetual Union between the
States. . .* Lancaster: Printed by
Francis Bailey. M,DCC,LXXVII.
26 p.

Clements Library

In spite of their weakness in forming a central government needed to carry on the Revolution, the Articles of Confederation did establish a variety of concepts vitally important to the later land ordinances and the separate but equal states from new territories. The *Articles* created a United States of America on a constitutional basis, provided for mutual citizenship among residents of all states, established national jurisdiction over boundaries, and designated a committee of nine states as empowered to modify the *Articles*. Precedence was set for administering additional territory.

In creating a government for the thirteen original colonies, the *Articles* were the first constitution of the United States. They were printed and sent to the newly designated states for ratification in 1777, but acceptance was delayed over the ownership of western lands. Seven states had claims based on original charters or Indian treaties.

Sovereignty was retained by the states, and Congress was their agent, entrusted with foreign affairs, Indian relations, and the postal service. The right of taxation was reserved to the states, which regardless of the number of delegates (two to seven) had but one vote in Congress. The central government had no judicial branch, only a weak executive, and could not regulate commerce. With experience, these were found to be fatal flaws.

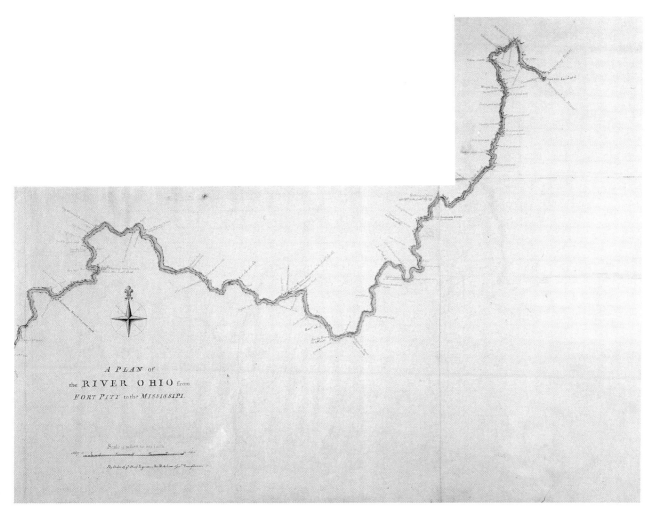

A PLAN of
the RIVER OHIO from
FORT PITT to the MISSISSIPI.

Scale 9 miles to an inch

By Order of ye Chief Engineer, Tho Hutchins Assis't Draughtsman

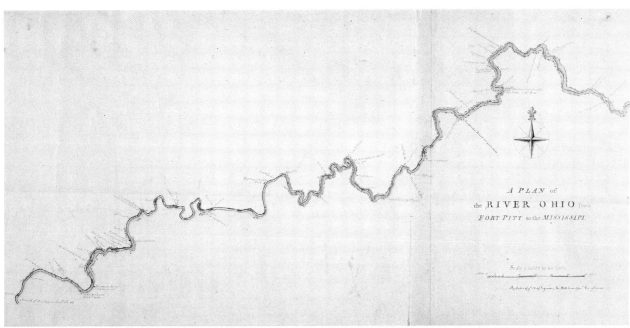

A PLAN of
the RIVER OHIO from
FORT PITT to the MISSISSIPI.

Scale 9 miles to an inch

By Order of ye Chief Engineer, Tho Hutchins Assis't Draughtsman

NWO-7

NWO-10.
Jonathan Carver, *Travels through the interior parts of North America in the years 1766, 1767, and 1768.* With *A New map of North America, from the latest discoveries 1778.* London: Printed for the author and sold by J. Walter, . . . and S. Crowder. MDCCLXXVIII. 543 p. Map, 14 1/8 x 21 3/8.

Lilly Library

Captain Carver, an American veteran of the French and Indian War, explored the area of modern Wisconsin, Lake Superior, Minnesota, and central Canada. His immensely popular book made both Englishmen and Americans conscious of the American West, and his map suggested possible political divisions around and below the Great Lakes. It was the prototype for the later printed maps.

NWO-11.

Blessed are the Peacemakers. London: Published by E. Darhery, Feb. 24, 1783. Political cartoon, 10 x 18.

Clements Library

Blessed are the, PEACE MAKERS

This British cartoon satirizes the opposition in Parliament to the preliminary peace treaty at the end of the Revolution because it was too favorable to America, France, and Spain. Lord Shelburne, the prime minister, accepted the fact that American independence was inevitable and had approved the treaty in order to lay a foundation for trade and cooperation between Britain and America. Canada was defined so that the Old Northwest and all land east of the Mississippi were recognized as part of the new United States of America.

The figures in the cartoon, left to right, represent Spain pushed along by France with a rope around the neck of King George III, followed by a satisfied Lord Shelburne with his rolled treaty and followed by America threatening Shelburne and the king with a harmless flail and dragging along a sulky Dutchman.

Parliament rejected the treaty, Shelburne had to resign, but the opposition formed a ministry that could negotiate no better treaty (after all Britain had lost the war), and the final treaty, 1783, differed little from what Shelburne had granted.

NWO-12.

By the United States in Congress Assembled, A Proclamation. Annapolis: Printed by John Dunlap. 1784. Broadside, 21 1/4 x 16 1/2.

Clements Library

This broadside is the first American printing of the definitive Treaty of Peace signed in Paris September 3, 1783, and ratified by Congress January 14, 1784. Charles Thomson, secretary, signed this copy. The United States were now firmly established in the international community of nations.

The treaty was signed by David Hartley for Great Britain, and by John Adams, Benjamin Franklin, and John Jay for the United States.

Congress chose Colonel Josiah Harmar of Pennsylvania as courier to carry the ratified copy of the treaty to Paris for exchange with Great Britain. Wind and weather delayed his coach and ship, and he did not arrive until March 29, 1784. Meanwhile Congress had ordered the government printer, John Dunlap, to strike off these broadsides.

By the UNITED STATES in CONGRESS Assembled,

A PROCLAMATION.

WHEREAS definitive articles of peace and friendship, between the United States of America and his Britannic majesty, were concluded and signed at Paris, on the 3d day of September, 1783, by the plenipotentiaries of the said United States, and of his said Britannic Majesty, duly and respectively authorized for that purpose; which definitive articles are in the words following.

In the Name of the Most Holy and Undivided
TRINITY.

IT having pleased the Divine Providence to dispose the hearts of the most serene and most potent Prince George the Third, by the Grace of God, King of Great-Britain, France and Ireland, Defender of the Faith, Duke of Brunswick and Lunenburg, Arch-Treasurer and Prince Elector of the Holy Roman Empire, &c. and of the United States of America, to forget all past misunderstandings and differences, that have unhappily interrupted the good correspondence and friendship which they mutually wish to restore; and to establish such a beneficial and satisfactory intercourse between the two countries, upon the ground of reciprocal advantages and mutual convenience, as may promote and secure to both perpetual peace and harmony: And having for this desirable end, already laid the foundation of peace and reconciliation, by the provisional articles, signed at Paris, on the 30th of November, 1782, by the commissioners empowered on each part, which articles were agreed to be inserted in, and to constitute the treaty of peace proposed to be concluded between the crown of Great-Britain and the said United States, but which treaty was not to be concluded until terms of peace should be agreed upon between Great-Britain and France, and his Britannic majesty should be ready to conclude such treaty accordingly; and the treaty between Great-Britain and France, having since been concluded, his Britannic majesty and the United States of America, in order to carry into full effect the provisional articles abovementioned, according to the tenor thereof, have constituted and appointed, that is to say, His Britannic majesty on his part, David Hartley, esquire, member of the parliament of Great-Britain, and the said United States on their part, John Adams, esquire, late a commissioner of the United States of America at the court of Versailles, late delegate in congress from the state of Massachusetts, and chief justice of the said state, and minister plenipotentiary of the said United States, to their high mightinesses the States General of the United Netherlands; Benjamin Franklin, esquire, late delegate in congress from the state of Pennsylvania, president of the convention of the said state, and minister plenipotentiary from the United States of America at the court of Versailles; John Jay, esquire, late president of congress, and chief justice of the state of New-York, and minister plenipotentiary from the said United States at the Court of Madrid, to be the plenipotentiaries for the concluding and signing the present definitive treaty; who after having reciprocally communicated their respective full powers, have agreed upon and confirmed the following articles.

ARTICLE 1st. His Britannic Majesty acknowledges the said United States, viz. New-Hampshire, Massachusetts-Bay, Rhode-Island and Providence Plantations, Connecticut, New-York, New-Jersey, Pennsylvania, Delaware, Maryland, Virginia, North-Carolina, South-Carolina and Georgia, to be free, sovereign and independent states: that he treats with them as such, and for himself, his heirs and successors, relinquishes all claims to the government, propriety and territorial rights of the same, and every part thereof:

ARTICLE. 2d. And that all disputes which might arise in future on the subject of the boundaries of the said United States may be prevented, it is hereby agreed and declared, that the following are and shall be their boundaries, viz.

From the north west angle of Nova-Scotia, viz. that angle which is formed by a line drawn due north from the source of Saint-Croix river to the Highlands; along the said Highlands which divide those rivers that empty themselves into the river Saint Lawrence from those which fall into the Atlantic Ocean, to the north-westernmost head of Connecticut river, thence down along the middle of that river to the forty-fifth degree of north latitude; from thence by a line due west on said latitude, until it strikes the river Iroquois or Cataraquy; thence along the middle of said river into lake Ontario, through the middle of said lake until it strikes the communication by water between that lake and lake Erie; thence along the middle of said communication into lake Erie, through the middle of said lake until it arrives at the water communication between that lake and lake Huron; thence along the middle of said water communication into the lake Huron; thence through the middle of said lake to the water communication between that lake and lake Superior; thence through lake Superior northward of the isles, Royal and Philipeaux to the long lake; thence through the middle of said long lake and the water communication between it and the lake of the Woods, to the said lake of the Woods; thence through the said lake to the most north-western point thereof, and from thence on a due west course to the river Mississippi; thence by a line to be drawn along the middle of the said river Mississippi, until it shall intersect the northernmost part of the thirty-first degree of north latitude. South by a line to be drawn due east from the determination of the line last mentioned, in the latitude of thirty-one degrees north of the equator, to the middle of the river Apalachicola or Catahouche; thence along the middle thereof to its junction with the Flint river; thence straight to the head of Saint Mary's river; and thence down along the middle of Saint Mary's river to the Atlantic Ocean. East by a line to be drawn along the middle of the river Saint-Croix, from its mouth in the bay of Fundy to its source, and from its source directly north to the aforesaid Highlands which divide the rivers that fall into the Atlantic Ocean from those which fall into the river Saint Lawrence; comprehending all islands within twenty leagues of any part of the shores of the United States, and lying between lines to be drawn due east from the points where the aforesaid boundaries between Nova-Scotia on the one part, and East Florida on the other, shall respectively touch the bay of Fundy, and the Atlantic Ocean; excepting such islands as now are or heretofore have been within the limits of the said province of Nova Scotia.

ARTICLE. 3d. It is agreed that the people of the United States shall continue to enjoy unmolested the right to take fish of every kind on the Grand Bank, and on all the other banks of Newfoundland; also in the gulph of Saint Lawrence, and at all other places in the sea, where the inhabitants of both countries used at any time heretofore to fish; and also that the inhabitants of the United States shall have liberty to take fish of every kind on such part of the coast of Newfoundland as, British fishermen shall use, (but not to dry or cure the same on that Island) and also on the coasts, bays and creeks of all other of his Britannic Majesty's dominions in America: and that the American fishermen shall have liberty to dry and cure fish in any of the unsettled bays, harbours and creeks of Nova-Scotia, Magdalen islands, and Labradore, so long as the same shall remain unsettled, but so soon as the same or either of them shall be settled, it shall not be lawful for the said fishermen to dry or cure fish at such settlement, without a previous agreement for that purpose with the inhabitants, proprietors or possessors of the ground.

ARTICLE 4th. It is agreed that creditors on either side, shall meet with no lawful impediment to the recovery of the full value in sterling money, of all bona fide debts heretofore contracted.

ARTICLE 5th. It is agreed that the Congress shall earnestly recommend it to the legislatures of the respective states, to provide for the restitution of all estates, rights and properties, which have been confiscated, belonging to real British subjects, and also of the estates, rights and properties of persons resident in districts in the possession of his majesty's arms, and who have not borne arms against the said United States. And that persons of any other description shall have free liberty to go to any part or parts of any of the Thirteen United States, and therein to remain twelve months unmolested in their endeavours to obtain the restitution of such of their estates, rights and properties, as may have been confiscated; and that Congress shall also earnestly recommend to the several states a reconsideration and revision of all acts or laws regarding the premises, so as to render the said laws or acts perfectly consistent, not only with justice and equity, but with that spirit of conciliation, which on the return of the blessings of peace should universally prevail. And that Congress shall also earnestly recommend to the several states, that the estates, rights and properties of such last mentioned persons shall be restored to them; they refunding to any persons who may be now in possession the bona fide price (where any has been given) which such persons may have paid on purchasing any of the said lands, rights or properties since the confiscation. And it is agreed that all persons who have any interest in confiscated lands, either by debts, marriage settlements, or otherwise, shall meet with no lawful impediment in the prosecution of their just rights.

ARTICLE 6th. That there shall be no future confiscations made, nor any prosecutions commenced against any person or persons for or by reason of the part which he or they may have taken in the present war; and that no person shall on that account, suffer any future loss or damage, either in his person liberty or property, and that those who may be in confinement on such charges, at the time of the ratification of the treaty in America, shall be immediately set at liberty, and the prosecutions so commenced be discontinued.

ARTICLE 7th. There shall be a firm and perpetual peace between his Britannic Majesty and the said States, and between the subjects of the one, and the citizens of the other, wherefore all hostilities both by sea and land shall from henceforth cease: all prisoners on both sides shall be set at liberty, and his Britannic Majesty shall with all convenient speed, and without causing any destruction, or carrying away any negroes or other property of the American inhabitants, withdraw all his armies, garrisons and fleets from the said United States and from every post place and harbour within the same; leaving in all fortifications the American artillery that may be therein, and shall also order and cause all archives, records deeds and papers, belonging to any of the said states, or their citizens, which in the course of the war may have fallen into the hands of his officers, to be forthwith restored and delivered to the proper states and persons to whom they belong.

ARTICLE 8th. The navigation of the river Mississippi, from its source to the Ocean, shall forever remain free and open to the subjects of Great-Britain and the citizens of the United States.

ARTICLE 9th. In case it should so happen that any place or territory belonging to Great-Britain or to the United States, should have been conquered by the arms of either from the other, before the arrival of the said provisional articles in America, it is agreed, that the same shall be restored without difficulty, and without requiring any compensation.

ARTICLE 10th. The solemn ratifications of the present treaty, expedited in good and due form, shall be exchanged between the contracting parties, in the space of six months, or sooner if possible, to be computed from the day of the signature of the present treaty. In witness whereof, we the undersigned, their ministers plenipotentiary, have in their name and in virtue of our full powers, signed with our hands the present definitive treaty, and caused the seals of our arms to be affixed thereto.

DONE at Paris, this third day of September, in the year of our Lord one thousand seven hundred and eighty-three.

(L. S.) D. HARTLEY, (L. S.) JOHN ADAMS,
(L. S.) B. FRANKLIN,
(L. S.) JOHN JAY.

AND we the United States in Congress assembled, having seen and duly considered the definitive articles aforesaid, did by a certain act under the seal of the United States, bearing date this 14th day of January 1784, approve, ratify and confirm the same and every part and clause thereof, engaging and promising that we would sincerely and faithfully perform and observe the same, and never suffer them to be violated by any one, or transgressed in any manner as far as should be in our power: and being sincerely disposed to carry the said articles into execution truly, honestly and with good faith, according to the intent and meaning thereof, we have thought proper by these presents, to notify the premises to all the good citizens of these United States, hereby requiring and enjoining all bodies of magistracy, legislative, executive and judiciary, all persons bearing office, civil or military, of whatever rank, degree or powers, and all others the good citizens of these States of every vocation and condition, that reverencing those stipulations entered into on their behalf, under the authority of that fœderal bond by which their existence as an independent people is bound up together, and is known and acknowledged by the nations of the world, and with that good faith which is every man's surest guide within their several offices jurisdictions and vocations, they carry into effect the said definitive articles, and every clause and sentence thereof, sincerely, strictly and completely.

GIVEN under the Seal of the United States, Witness his Excellency THOMAS MIFFLIN, our President, at Annapolis, this fourteenth day of January, in the year of our Lord one thousand seven hundred and eighty-four, and of the sovereignty and independence of the United States of America the eighth.

Cha Thomson secy

ANNAPOLIS: Printed by JOHN DUNLAP, Printer for the United States in Congress assembled.

NWO-12

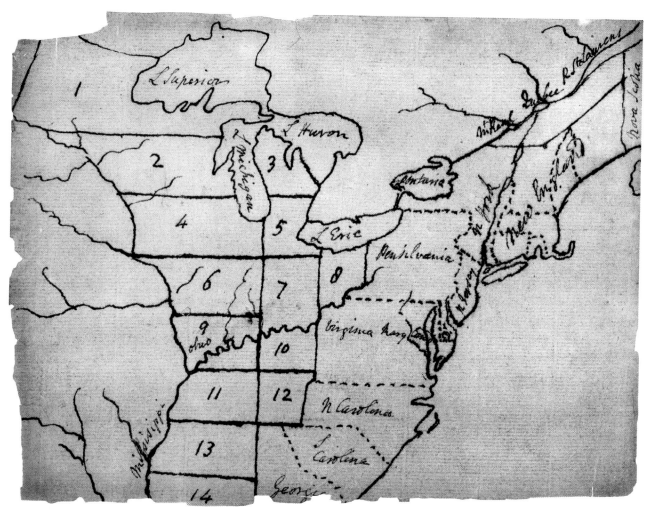

NWO-13.
"Map of the eastern half of the United States, 1784." Manuscript map, 7 x 9.

This small map represents preliminary thinking about the division of the western lands won by the Americans. It was found in the papers of David Hartley, Lord Shelburne's diplomatic agent in negotiating the preliminary peace treaty with the American colonies in 1782 and who served the opposition government in the same capacity in 1783. Hartley transmitted a copy of the plan to London on January 9, 1785, and kept a copy for himself. Presumably he obtained the map in Paris from Thomas Jefferson who arrived there as our ambassador on August 6, 1784. No original in Jefferson's hand is known to exist, however.

Jefferson had served since February 1784 as chairman of a congressional committee to prepare a plan for temporary government of the western territory. In the report submitted to Congress the committee did not specify fourteen new states, but did give names for ten of them, which must have come from the classical mind of Jefferson:

Sylvania	Illinoia
Michigania	Saratoga
Cherronesus	Polypotamia
Assenisipia	Pelisipia
Metropotamia	Washington

28

NWO-14.
William Faden, *The United States of North America, with the British & Spanish Territories according to the Treaty.* [London,] 1783. colored map, 24 x 27.

See illustration on page 20

Clements Library

This detailed and accurate map of the eastern two-thirds of North America revealed the immense expanse of land of the new United States. England retained Canada above the Great Lakes, and Spain reacquired East and West Florida, which connected with Spanish Louisiana.

What the map does not show is that England kept its troops at Fort Niagara, Fort Detroit, and Mackinac Island and enjoyed a continuing fur trade with Indians simply because the United States had no troops available to take over those posts. The potential for western development was there, however.

NWO-15.
[United States Continental Congress. Committee report on Virginia's conditional cession of its claims to land northwest of the Ohio River, 1781.] Broadside, 17 x 13.

Clements Library

Seven states had claims to western lands, based on original charters or Indian treaties: Massachusetts, Connecticut, Virginia, Maryland, North Carolina, South Carolina, and Georgia. Maryland urged that they turn over their claims to the central government, which could do nothing about them until the separate claims were extinguished. In early 1781, Virginia offered a conditional cession of its claim to land northwest of the Ohio: the land ceded should be formed into states, the titles granted to the French and Canadian inhabitants of Kaskaskia and Vincennes should be confirmed, 150,000 acres should be reserved for members of Colonel George Rogers Clark's expedition against those posts in 1778-79, other lands reserved as bonuses for Virginia troops be recognized, and deeds to this land granted by Indians to private persons should be voided.

The committee recommended acceptance of Virginia's conditions, except for an unnecessary one. This broadside report is obviously a working copy by one committee member.

NWO-16.
The Grand committee. . . to whom were. . . referred a motion of Mr. Monroe, respecting the cessions and division of western lands and territory, -report. . . [Annapolis?] 1785. Broadside, 8 x 13.

Clements Library

This report, adopted by Congress, asked Virginia and Massachusetts to remove any restrictions on their western lands ceded to the United States that might hinder the intention to divide the territory into "not less than two, nor more than five" states. This was the first official declaration of the number of states that might be formed in the Old Northwest. The number was changed in 1787 to not less than three or more than five states. The original thirteen states did not want the Northwest Territory broken up into so many future states that they would rival the powers of the original states in the general government.

NWO-17.
"Articles of a Treaty concluded at Fort McIntosh this 21st day of January 1785." Manuscript copy, 4 p.

Josiah Harmar paper, Clements Library

In the treaty ending the American Revolution, Great Britain ignored lands claimed by their Indian allies, leaving the United States to deal with them. The Indians were resentful of their recent allies and hostile to the Americans. This treaty was held at Fort McIntosh, on the Ohio River northwest of Pittsburgh at the mouth of Beaver Creek.

The negotiations forced certain chiefs of the Wyandot or Huron, the Delaware, Chippewa, and Ottawa nations, who were now "under the protection of the United States," to confine themselves to a strip of Ohio land between the Cuyahoga and Great Miami rivers, about one-quarter of the future state. Detroit and Mackinac Island were "reserved to the sole use of the United States," as was the area surrounding the grant to the Indians. No white settlers could occupy the land given to the Indians. Payment was made in cash and trade goods to the several tribes. Only the year before the chiefs of the various western tribes had met and agreed not to surrender any land to the United States; consequently there was widespread dissatisfaction with this treaty, and the same land sales had to be renegotiated four times.

NWO-18.
"By the United States in Congress assembled April 1st, 7th, 12th, 1785." Manuscript copy, 3 p.

Josiah Harmar papers, Clements Library

Pennsylvania troops had been sent to Fort McIntosh as escorts to the United States commissioners who negotiated the treaty with the Indians (item 17). Reactions to the treaty among other Indians clearly indicated that troops would soon be needed to protect the frontier and the surveyors mapping the area to make possible deeding the land to settlers. Reluctantly and contrary to Congressional opposition to a standing army, the Congress enacted three resolutions in April 1785 to recreate a regular national army of 700 men (one regiment) to be drawn from four States: Connecticut, New York, New Jersey, and Pennsylvania. Colonel Josiah Harmar of the latter state was made commander.

NWO-19.
[Petition of Ohio settlers to delay eviction, addressed to] Col. Josiah Harmar, April 15, 1785. Manuscript copy, 2 p.

Josiah Harmar papers, Clements Library

Not only were Indians going to be a problem in the Northwest Territory. White settlers, impatient to claim land beyond the Ohio River, had already "squatted" on the land without a deed or any payment. Congress had ordered their eviction, and Colonel Harmar had given them notice of their illegal status, which they could not deny. This petition to Colonel Harmar by sixty-one squatters asked for a delay of eviction until they heard from their direct appeal to Congress over their distressed condition and the need for time to build other dwellings and relocate. Harmar was sympathetic to their polite appeal and their promise to obey Congress's decision.

The problem of squatters did not go away. Their settlement on land to which they had no title confused legitimate purchasers later and, of course, antagonized the Indians.

NWO-20.

By the United States in Congress assembled. . . May 20, 1785, an Ordinance for ascertaining the mode of disposing of Lands in the Western Territory. Hartford: Printed by Hudson and Goodwin. [1785.] 4 p.

Clements Library

By the UNITED STATES in CONGRESS *Assembled.*
APRIL 23, 1784.
RESOLVED,

THAT so much of the territory ceded, or to be ceded by individual states, to the United States, as is already purchased, or shall be purchased, of the Indian inhabitants, and offered for sale by Congress, shall be divided into distinct states in the following manner, as nearly such cessions will admit; that is to say, by parallels of latitude, so that each state shall comprehend from north to south two degrees of latitude, beginning to count from the completion of thirty-five degrees north of the equator; and by meridians of longitude, one of which shall pass through the lowest point of the rapids of Ohio, and the other through the western cape of the mouth of the great Kanhaway; but the territory eastward of this last meridian, between the Ohio, lake Erie, and Pensylvania, shall be one state, whatsoever may be its comprehension of latitude. That which may lie beyond the completion of the forty-fifth degree between the said meridians shall make part of the state adjoining it on the south; and that part of the Ohio, which is between the same meridians coinciding nearly with the parallel of thirty-nine degrees, shall be substituted so far in lieu of that parallel as a boundary line.

That the settlers on any territory so purchased and offered for sale, shall, either on their own motion, or on the order of Congress, receive authority from them, with appointments of time and place, for their free males of full age, within the limits of their state, to meet together, for the purpose of establishing a temporary government, to adopt the constitution and laws of any one of the original states; so that laws nevertheless shall be subject to alteration by their primary legislature; and to erect, subject to a like alteration, counties, townships, or other divisions, for the election of members for their legislature.

That when any such state shall have acquired twenty thousand free inhabitants, on giving due proof thereof to Congress, they shall receive from them authority, with appointments of time and place, to call a convention of representatives, to establish a permanent constitution and government for themselves. Provided that both the temporary and permanent governments be established on their principles as their basis.

FIRST. That they shall for ever remain a part of this confederacy of the United States of America.

SECOND. That they shall be subject to the articles of confederation in all those cases, in which the original states shall be so subject; and to all the acts and ordinances of the United States in Congress assembled, conformable thereto.

THIRD. That they shall in no case shall interfere with the primary disposal of the soil by the United States in Congress assembled; nor with the ordinances and regulations which Congress may find necessary for securing the title in such soil to the bona fide purchasers.

FOURTH. That they shall be subject to pay a part of the federal debts, contracted or to be contracted; to be apportioned on them by Congress, according to the same common rule and measure by which apportionments thereof shall be made on the other states.

FIFTH. That no tax shall be imposed on lands the property of the United States.

SIXTH. That their respective governments shall be republican.

SEVENTH. That the lands of non-resident proprietors shall in no case be taxed higher than those of residents within any new state, before the admission thereof to a voce by its delegates in Congress.

That whensoever any of the said states shall have of free inhabitants, as many as shall then be in one, the least numerous, of the thirteen original states, such state shall be admitted by its delegates into the Congress of the United States, on an equal footing with the said original states; provided the consent of so many states in Congress is first obtained as may at the time be competent to such admission. And in order to adapt the said articles of confederation to the state of Congress, when its number shall be thus encreased, it shall be proposed to the legislatures of the several originally parties thereto, to require the assent of two thirds of the United States in Congress assembled, in all those cases, wherein by the said articles, the assent of nine states is now required; which being agreed to by them, shall be binding on the new states. Until such admission by their delegates into Congress, any of the said states after the establishment of their temporary government shall have authority to keep a member in Congress, with a right of debating, but not of voting.

That measures not inconsistent with the principles of the confederation, and necessary for the preservation of peace and good order among the settlers, in any of the said new states, until they assume a temporary government as aforesaid, may from time to time be taken by the United States in Congress assembled.

That the preceding articles shall be formed into a charter of compact; shall be duly executed by the president of the United States in Congress assembled, under his hand, and the seal of the United States; shall be promulgated; and shall stand as fundamental constitutions between the thirteen original states, and each of the several states now newly described, unalterable from and

---

The land Ordinance of 1784 was never implemented before it was superseded by the Ordinance of 1785. The latter was primarily designed to raise revenue toward payment of the public debt by selling land in the Old Northwest as soon as the Indians relinquished their claims and it was surveyed. This Hartford printing includes both Ordinances.

The Ordinance of 1785 served as the primary legislation for a public land system. It called for a survey with a base line beginning at the point where the Ohio River intersected the western boundary of Pennsylvania and extending west for seven ranges (42 miles) and then south. Townships six miles square were made up of thirty-six sections, each one mile square (640 acres). Three sections of each township were reserved for public school use, another section for religious use, and other lands reserved for Continental officers, Canadian refugees, Virginia soldiers, and Christian Indians per agreement with Virginia (item 15). The land was to be sold at public auctions for not less than one dollar an acre, and certificates of pay to Revolutionary veterans would be acceptable at face value. Still needed was a process by which government would be established over this territory.

NWO-21.

"Township No. VII Range No. XIV" Meigs County, Ohio c. 1787. Colored manuscript map, 15 x 12.

See illustration on page 37

Clements Library

This map shows how a given township was laid out in thirty-six sections. The reserves are indicated, two creeks are shown, hills are marked, and the quality of the land is labeled. Some sections are broken up into two or three parts, the smaller tracts being more affordable to many individuals. The map bears the signature of Rufus Putnam, one of the founders of the Ohio Company and later Surveyor General of the United States. He probably made this survey himself.

The three sections reserved for future sale by Congress were held until the price might well increase above a dollar an acre. It was always section sixteen, near the center, whose sale would help support a public school. Another section was sold for religious purposes, presumably a church building or to attract a minister to locate there.

NWO-22.

Thomas Hutchins to Col. Josiah Harmar, August 13, 1786, at camp on the Ohio River near the Pennsylvania line. Autograph letter signed, 2 p.

Josiah Harmar papers, Clements Library

The survey of the Northwest Territory began in September 1785 under Thomas Hutchins, who had mapped the Ohio River in 1766 (item 7). He was now Geographer of the United States. He was assisted by deputy surveyors and protected by a company of troops. Bad weather, rugged terrain, and threats from Indians made surveying in the wilderness both slow and hazardous. After two years the total land surveyed amounted to only 675,000 acres. Between 1785 and 1816 only parts of the present states of Ohio, Indiana, Illinois, and Michigan were surveyed and available for sale.

Impatient to derive some revenue, Congress authorized sale of some surveyed lands at public auction in New York City from September 21 to October 9, 1787. The result was disappointing: only 72,900 acres sold and the money received was largely in depreciated paper money. This experience persuaded Congress to consider making large sales to land companies.

NWO-23.

Manasseh Cutler, *A Map of the Federal Territory from the western boundary of Pennsylvania to the Scioto River...* Boston, 1788. 28 1/2 x 21.

Clements Library

Cutler was a minister, physician, lawyer, botanist, and one of the founders of the Ohio Company. He received his information in New York from Thomas Hutchins and his surveyors. He also issued late in 1787 at Salem, ahead of the map, a pamphlet that was enthusiastic about prospects in the Northwest in order to promote land sales. Cutler himself did not get out to Marietta, Ohio, until summer 1788, the town having been founded opposite Fort Harmar in April by a party under Rufus Putnam.

The map shows the land surveyed in the seven ranges, the adjoining tract purchased by the Ohio Company (not yet surveyed), the Scioto plains reserved for Virginia, and the Western Reserve claimed by Connecticut. The sale to the Scioto Company of land west of Virginia's holding is not indicated. The small squares in each township are mile-square sections.

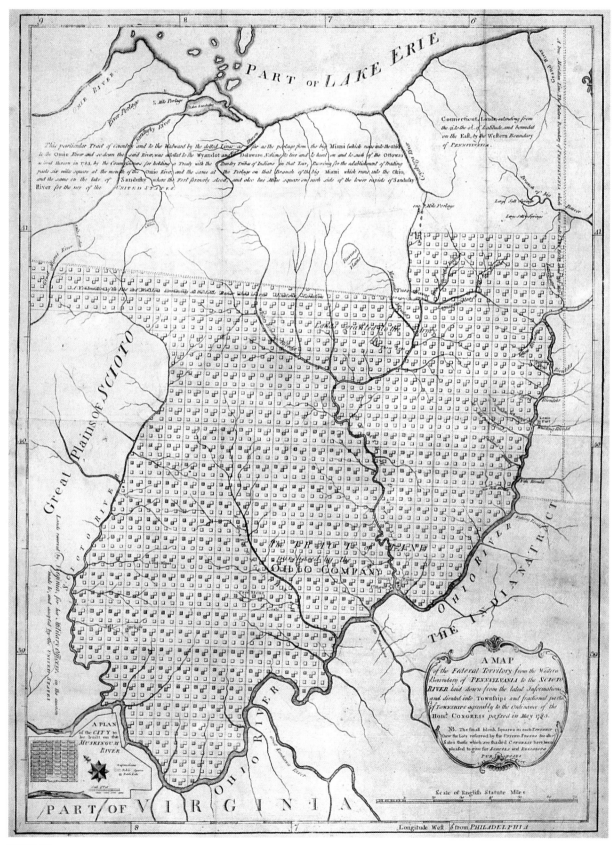

NWO-23

NWO-24.
An Ordinance for the Government of the Territory of the United States, North-West of the River Ohio, July 13, 1787. Signed by Chas. Thomson, secy. 2 p. 2 copies.

See illustration on page 6

Clements Library
Lilly Library

The famous Northwest Ordinance prescribed the stages of government to be followed by any given area in order to become a state and guaranteed certain rights of the inhabitants. First, Congress would appoint a governor, a secretary, and three judges to adopt suitable laws necessary to administer the territory. As soon as 5,000 adult males were counted in a given territory, they could elect a general assembly, which would meet and elect a legislative council of ten members, five of whom Congress would appoint to that office. Thereafter the governor, legislative council, and house of representatives would make laws for the district and elect a non-voting delegate to Congress. After adoption of the Constitution, they were appointed by the President, with the consent of the Senate.

The following articles were considered to be in effect and unalterable: freedom of religion, trial by jury, sanctity of contracts and private property, good faith observed toward the Indians, and slavery prohibited throughout the territory. Perhaps the most famous article is the third, that begins: "Religion, morality and knowledge, being necessary to good government and the happiness of mankind, schools and the means of education shall forever be encouraged." Hence the provision in the land Ordinance of 1785 for one section in each township to be sold for school purposes.

As a result of this Ordinance the United States solved the problem of "colonies" which had baffled Great Britain, by allowing new territories to form into states and be admitted to the Union on an equal footing with the original thirteen states. Thirty-one of our fifty states were carved out of the public domain under the basic pattern of the Ordinance of 1787. By contrast, the British empire was static: colonies could never evolve into equal status with Great Britain.

The two copies show both pages of the printed Ordinance.

NWO-25.
Nathan Dane to Rufus King, July 16, 1787, New York. Autograph letter signed, 3 p.

State Historical Society
of Wisconsin

Three days after passage of the Northwest Ordinance, Dane wrote to his friend and listed the committee of Congress that prepared it: Edward Carrington and Richard Henry Lee of Virginia, Melancton Smith of New York, John Kean of South Carolina, and himself of Massachusetts.

Dane also revealed that he might be considered the principal author of the document. "We met several times and at last agreed on some principles, at least Lee, Smith & myself. . . when I drew the ordinance which passed (a few words excepted) as I originally formed it. . ." He admitted he was surprised by the ease with which the Congress accepted the prohibition of slavery in the Territory. He mentioned the pending sale to the Ohio Company (see below) of a large chunk of the Northwest Territory as a quick way of raising money for war debts.

NWO-26.
*Articles of an Association by the
Name of the Ohio Company.*
Worcester: Isaiah Thomas.
MDCCLXXXVI, 12 p.

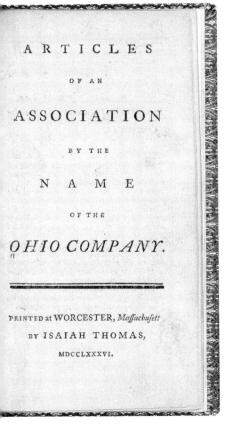

ARTICLES

OF AN

ASSOCIATION

BY THE

NAME

OF THE

OHIO COMPANY.

PRINTED at WORCESTER, *Maſſachuſetⁱ*
BY ISAIAH THOMAS,
MDCCLXXXVI.

The Ohio Company was organized at Boston in March 1786 at the instigation of Manasseh Cutler, Rufus Putnam, Benjamin Tupper, Winthrop Sargent, Thomas H. Cushing, and John Brooks, all New Englanders. It was a stock company with a capital of a million dollars in continental certificates issued as pay to veterans of the Revolution. Its purpose was to buy land northwest of the Ohio River and resell it to settlers. Following another meeting in March 1787, Cutler was sent to New York City to lobby for the land purchase with Congress. He arrived a few days before the Ordinance of 1787 was reported out of committee and offered his opinion thereon. A mode of government for the Territory would make the area more attractive to settlers.

On July 24 Cutler made an offer on behalf of the Ohio Company and ran into opposition. But Congress ordered the Board of Treasury to "Close the Contract," which was done on October 27, 1787. The Ohio Company received 1,500,000 acres extending westward and southward from Marietta, at the mouth of the Muskingum. The currency used for payment was so depreciated that Congress actually received only eight cents an acre. An additional 5,000,000 acres, when surveyed, was made available on installments to the Scioto Company, the company being a cover for various Congressmen and other government officials legally prevented from speculating in Ohio lands. The option was taken in the names of Cutler and Sargent.

NWO-27.
"Plan of the Ohio Company's Purchase." Colored manuscript map c. 1787, 10 1/4 x 7 7/8.

This is a contemporary map of land sold to the Ohio Company as surveyed into townships. It starts at the mouth of the Muskingum River and extends down the Ohio River past the Kanawha to Symmes Creek. Marietta, founded in 1788, is not shown. For whom the map was made is not known.

NWO-28.

Treasury Department, July 20th, 1790. . . the secretary of the treasury respectfully reports,. . . [Philadelphia, 1790.] 4 p.

Clements Library

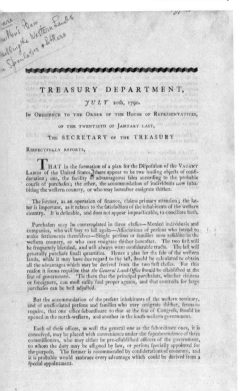

After the adoption of the Constitution, Alexander Hamilton became Secretary of the Treasury and found western lands one of the few major sources of income for the new federal government. The immediate problem was whether to maximize income by selling to speculators—that is, to rich individuals or companies that would buy large tracts or to individuals or associations of them who would settle on the land and could afford only modest acreage.

In this document Hamilton reported to the House of Representatives the policy choices. If settlers were to be encouraged, two land offices needed to be established in the Northwest and Southwest, besides the one at the seat of government in Philadelphia. Moreover, the minimum size of the sale to an individual settler should be reduced to one hundred acres at thirty cents an acre, with twenty-five percent down. A surveyor general should be appointed along with a superintendent of the general land office. Large tracts could be sold also. Purchasers should bear the cost of surveys. Hamilton's recommendations were favored by the House, but did not pass the Senate. The public land policy was not revised until 1796.

NWO-29.

An Act for granting Lands to the inhabitants and settlers of Vincennes and the Illinois country, in the territory northwest of the Ohio, and for confirming them in their possessions, March 3, 1791. [Philadelphia: Printed by Francis Childs and John Swain. 1791.] [2]p.

Lilly Library

The territory northwest of the Ohio River was not a vacant area when the Confederation Congress began selling parcels to American settlers and companies. Certain French-Canadian residents had been there for generations, and there were three towns, established by Moravian missionaries, of Christian Indians on the Muskingum River. It seemed only fair to furnish these occupants with proper deeds, and the new government under the Constitution acted in March 1791 to provide them. Grants were limited to no more than 400 acres. The act was signed by Thomas Jefferson as Secretary of State.

This copy bears the autograph of Samuel Huntington, once governor of Connecticut and a signer of the Declaration of Independence. The French inhabitants did not adapt to the frontier agricultural economy (they were mainly traders) and most of them sold their claims to Americans.

SCALE of forty chains to an inch

N.º 36 640 Acres John Burnham	N.º 30 640 Acres John Burnham	N.º 24 640 Acres Nath.ᵉˡ Whitmore	N.º 18 640 Acres Nath.ᵉˡ Whitmore	N.º 12 640 Acres Benj.ⁿ Wadsworth	N.º 6 640 Acres Benj.ⁿ Wadsworth

Lick

N.º 35 640 Acres John Burnham of Lynnfield	N.º 29 640 Acres Ministry	N.º 23 640 Acres Jn.º Treadwell	N.º 17 640 Acres John Treadwell	N.º 11 640 Acres Congress	N.º 5 640 Acres Nath.ᵉˡ Brown

N.º 34 640 Acres Benj.ⁿ Wadsworth	N.º 35 262 Acres / N.º 31 262 Acres	N.º 23 262 Acres / N.º 17 262 Acres	N.º 16 640 Acres School	N.º 5 262 Acres / N.º 4 262 Acres	N.º 4 640 Acres Mathew Park Elijah Shoap

N.º 29 262 Acres — N.º 18 262 Acres

N.º 33 640 Acres Peter Oliver	N.º 33 262 Acres / N.º 32 362 Acres	N.º 29 262 Acres	N.º 36 / N.º 6 262 Acres	N.º 2 262 Acres / N.º 2 262 Acres	N.º 3 640 Acres Will.ᵐ Pierce

N.º 31 262 Acres / N.º 1 262 Acres

Fine white clay

N.º 32 640 Acres Joseph William	N.º 26 640 Acres Congress	N.º 25 262 Acres / N.º 19 262 Acres	N.º 7 262 Acres / N.º 13 262 Acres	N.º 8 640 Acres Congress	N.º 2 640 Acres Will.ᵐ Pierce

N.º 31 640 Acres John Safford	N.º 25 640 Acres Obadiah Parsons	N.º 19 640 Acres W.ᵐ Cleveland	N.º 13 640 Acres John Burnham	N.º 1 640 Acres Mass.º Cutler	N.º 1 640 Acres Mass.º Cutler

N.B. The fractions or lots of 262 acres bear the same number as the mile squares or sections to which they are annexed.—
Each lot lies for the quantity of acres marked, but in many instances does not hold out measure.—

In Ohio company's purchase. A copy.

+ First quality of upland & standing alone supposed land level.
‡ Middle or second quality of upland when alone supposed land level.
⌇ Streams of water & the figures in red ink their width in links.
↑ Ridge or long hill of gradual ascent.
* Bottom or interval land.
ǂ Hills short & steep.
/ Hilly ridgy broken poor land.
+ Stones & ledges of rocks.
↑ Springs of water.
P Red paint.

Rufus Putnam

NWO-21

TENS-QUA-TA-WA

or THE ONE THAT OPENS THE DOOR

Shawnese Prophet

Brother of Tecumthe

Painted for Gov. Lewis Cass by J. O. Lewis at Detroit 1823.

NWO-46

NWO-48

NWO-30.
Henry Knox to Brig. Gen. Josiah
Harmar, August 24th, 1790, War
Department. Manuscript letter
signed, 4 p.

Josiah Harmar papers,
Clements Library

The Secretary of War advised Harmar that Governor Arthur St. Clair and President Washington had approved of an expedition against the Miami Indians on the Maumee River, and he should move as soon as possible. Knox emphasized the importance of success and the prevention of surprise on the part of the Indians.

With a force of 320 regulars and 1,133 militia from Kentucky and Pennsylvania, some of them mounted, Harmar set out northward from Fort Washington (Cincinnati) on September 30, 1790. The contractors who furnished supplies performed poorly and he had little forage for his horses. The expedition was not harassed during its march to Kekionga, the Miami capital at modern Fort Wayne, and half a dozen other villages nearby, including Delaware and Shawnee towns. The villages were all deserted. Harmar burned them and their big cornfields on October 17. Little Turtle, chief of the Miami, observed all this destruction.

Feeling confident, Harmar ordered Colonel Hardin of the militia to scout the area westward with 180 militia and 30 regulars. He marched his men into an ambush. Only eight of the regulars survived and the militia lost about forty men as they fled. Harmar decided to turn back south on October 21. Colonel Hardin persuaded Harmar to let him return and take revenge on the Indians. He led 340 militia and 60 regulars, under the overall command of Major John Willys, a regular officer. Little Turtle quickly devised another ambush. Major Willys and fifty of the regulars were killed and about seventy-five of the militia lost their lives. The Miami loss is unknown, but heavy enough to prevent any pursuit of Harmar on his return to Fort Washington. He believed his expedition had been a success. No one else did, as it only encouraged the Indians to make more raids on frontier families. Congress authorized a court of inquiry, which absolved Harmar of misconduct, but he resigned. Command of the militia forces passed to Governor St. Clair.

NWO-31.
The Columbian Tragedy: containing a particular and official Account of the. . . Bloody Indian Battle. . . Boston, 1792. Broadside, 22 x 17.

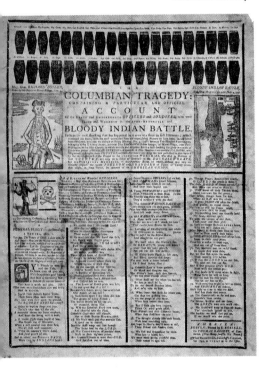

Although the British had concluded peace with the United States in 1783 and abandoned their Indian allies, they were not averse to encouraging their natural hostility to American troops and to settlers pushing westward. After taking a heavy toll of Harmar's expedition in 1790, they were ready to meet a second expedition the next year under Governor Arthur St. Clair. Near modern Fort Recovery, Ohio, on the Indiana line, above Greeneville, they surprised St. Clair's encampment of 3,000 men, killing 630 and wounding 283, who were left behind. It was the most severe defeat ever suffered by American arms. Again, Little Turtle commanded the Indians.

British officials in Canada promised the Indians that the United States would have to agree to creation of an Indian buffer state between Detroit and the Ohio River, nullifying earlier treaties with the Indians and wiping out the Northwest Territory.

The thirty-nine coffins are labeled for the officers killed. The ballad was probably composed by the printer's wife.

NWO-32.
Laws passed in the Territory of the United States north-west of the River Ohio, from the commencement of the government to the 31st of December, 1791. Philadelphia: Printed by Francis Childs and John Swaine. M,DCC,XCII. 74 p.

The five officials appointed by Congress to govern the Northwest Territory relied on the three judges to adopt laws from the older states to cover the needs of inhabitants. They "adapted" laws as well as "adopted" them exactly, a practice to which Governor St. Clair objected, as did certain local lawyers. Nevertheless, Congress authorized publication in 1792 of all the laws in force in the Territory. This first territorial code was printed in Philadelphia and distributed to lawyers in general. It was evidence that order and legal procedures now existed in the former wilderness.

NWO-33.
The Centinel of the North-Western Territory, vol. I, num. 1, November 9, 1793, Cincinnati, 2 p.

The issue of the first newspaper to appear in the Northwest Territory provided further evidence that "culture" was rising there. Settlers were fast reproducing the amenities of a civilization to which they had become accustomed back East.

THE
CENTINEL of the *North-Western* TERRITORY.

Open to all parties—but influenced by none.

(Vol. I.)   SATURDAY, *November 9, 1793.*   (Num. I.)

The *Printer* of the CENTINEL of the *North-Western TERRITORY*, to the *Public*.

HAVING arrived at *Cincinnati*, he has applied himself to that which has been the principal object of his removal to this country, the Publication of a *News-Paper*.

This country is in its infancy, and the inhabitants are daily exposed to an enemy who, not content with taking away the lives of men in the field, have swept away whole families, and burnt their habitations. We are well aware that the want of a regular and certain trade down the Missisippi, deprives this country in a great measure, of money at the present time. These are discouragements, nevertheless I am led to believe the people of this country are disposed to promote science, and have the fullest assurance that the *Press* from its known utility will receive proper encouragement. And on my part am content with small gains, at the present, flattering myself that from attention to business, I shall deserve the good wishes of those who have already countenanced me in this undertaking, and secure the friendship of subsequent population.

It is to be hoped that the CENTINEL will prove of great utility to the people of this Country, not only to inform them of what is going on in the east of the Atlantic in arms, and in arts of peace—but what more particularly concerns us, the different transactions of the states in the union, and especially of our own Territory, at so great a distance from the seat of general government—it is a particular grievance, that the people have not been acquainted with the proceedings of the legislature of the union, in which they are as much interested, as any part of the United States.— It is expected the CENTINEL, will in a great measure remedy this misfortune.

These are substantial advantages, which will result from the publication of this *paper* ; but it must be an agreeable amusement to know a thousand particulars which make up the intelligence, though not so immediately interesting to the property & persons of men, whether they be of a philosophical, political, historical or moral nature.

The EDITOR therefore rests his success on the merits of the publication, but as an inducement to the people of this country, to make exertions to support the *Press*, he must observe that they will have an opportunity, by means of this *paper* to make themselves and their situations known abroad; if they have valuable lands to dispose of, it can be made known ; if they have grievences to lay before the public, it can now be done. I hope therefore, all men of public spirit will consider the undertaking as a proper object of attention, and not consult merely their own personal interest, but the interest of the public and the coming time.

The MONK.
CALAIS.

A POOR monk of the order of St. Francis came into the room to beg something for his convent. No man cares to have his virtues the sport of contingencies— or one man may be generous, as another man is puissant—*sed non, quo ad hanc*—or be as it may—for there is no regular reasoning upon the ebbs and flows of our humours ; they may depend upon the same causes, for ought I know, which influence the tides themselves—'twould oft be no discredit to us suppose it was so ; I'm sure at least for myself, that in many a case I should be more highly satisfied, to have it said by the world, "I had an affair with the moon, in which there was neither sin nor shame," than have it pass altogether as my own act and deed, wherein there was so much of both.

—But be this as it may. The moment I cast my eyes upon him, I was predetermined not to give him a single sous, and accordingly I put my purse into my pocket—buttoned it up—set myself a little more upon my center, and advanced up gravely to him: there was something I fear forbidding in my look: I have his figure this moment before my eyes, and think there was that in it which deserved better.

The monk, as I judged from the break in his tonsure, a few scatter'd white hairs upon his temples being all that remained of it, might be about seventy—but from his eyes, and that sort of fire which was in them, which seemed more temper'd by courtesy than years, could be no more than sixty—Truth might lie between—He was certainly sixty-five ; and the general air of his countenance, notwithstanding something seemed to have been planting wrinkles in it before their time, agreed to the account.

It was one of those heads, which Guido has often painted—mild, pale—penetrating, free from all common place ideas of fat-contented ignorance, looking downwards upon the earth—it look'd forwards; but look'd as if it look'd at something beyond this world. How one of his order came by it, heaven above, who let it fall upon a monk's shoulders, best knows ; but it would have suited a Bramin, and had I met it upon the plains of Indostan, I had reverenced it.

The rest of his outline may be given in a few strokes ; one might put it into the hands of any one to design, for 'twas neither elegant nor otherwise, but as character and expression made it so : it was a thin, spare form, something above the common size, if it lost not the distinction by a bend forwards in the figure—but it was the attitude of entreaty ; and as it now stands presented to my imagination, it gained more than it lost by it.

When he had enter'd the room three paces, he stood still ; and laying his left hand upon his breast, (a slender white staff with which he journey'd being in his right)—when I had got close up to him, he introduced himself with the little story of the wants of his convent, and the poverty of his order —and did it with so simple a grace—and such an air of deprecation was there in the whole cast of his look and figure—I was bewitched not to have been struck with it——

—A better reason was, I had predetermined not to give him a single sous.

——'Tis very true, said I, replying to a cast upwards with his eyes, with which he had ...... address—'tis very true ...... and hea ...... ires who have no other but ...... charity, ... world, the stock of which, I fear, is no way ...... icient for the many *great claims* which are hourly made upon it.

As I pronounced the words *great claims*, he gave a slight glance with his eye downwards upon the sleeve of his tunic—I felt the full force of the appeal—I acknowledge it, said I —a coarse habit, and that but once in three years, with meagre diet—are no great matters ; and the true point of pity is, as they can be earn'd in the world with so little industry, that your order should wish to procure them by pressing upon a fund which is the property of the lame, the blind, the aged, and the infirm—the captive who lies down counting over and over again the days of his afflictions, languishes also for his share of it ; and had you been of the *order of Mercy*, instead of the order of St. Francis, poor as I am, continued I, pointing at my portmanteau, full cheerfully should it have been open'd to you, for the ransom of the unfortunate —The monk made me a bow—but of all others, resumed I, the unfortunate of our own country, surely, have the first right ; and I have left thousands in distress upon our own shore—— The monk gave a cordial wave with his head —as much as to say, No doubt there is misery enough in every corner of the world, as well as within our convent.—But we distinguish, said I, laying my hand upon the sleeve of his tunic, in return for his appeal—we distinguish, my good father ! betwixt those who ...

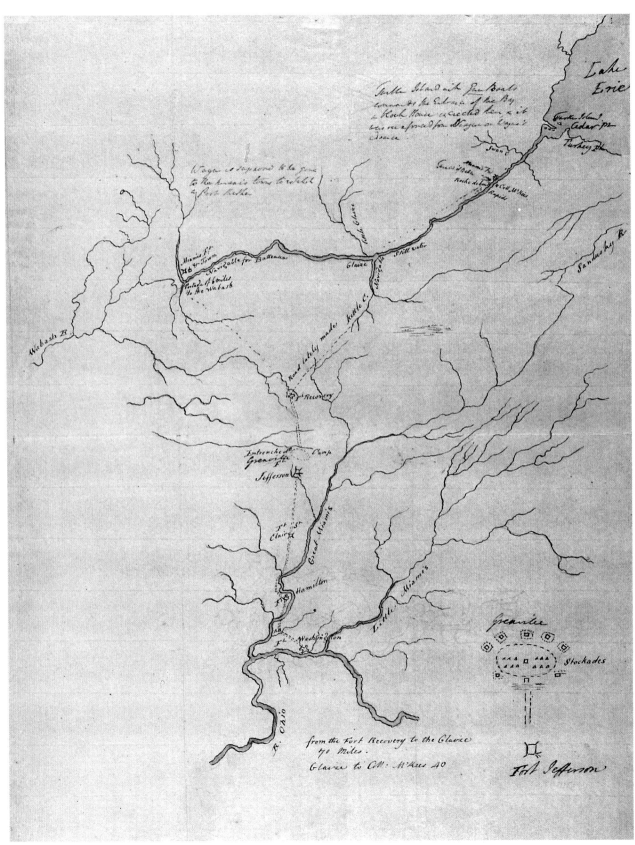

Continued Indian raids led to Major General Anthony Wayne's appointment as commander of the small United States Army and its augmentation with militia. Wayne trained his troops in wilderness fighting for two years before seeking to fight the Indians. He marched north from Fort Washington (Cincinnati) on October 7, 1793, toward the Maumee River. At the site of St. Clair's defeat, he built Fort Recovery and wintered near there. The Indians were impressed, just as Wayne intended. At the same time, John Graves Simcoe, the British governor of Upper Canada, was ordered to build Fort Miamis about five miles from the mouth of the Maumee, clearly on American soil. The fort was meant to encourage Indian resistance, and active assistance was promised.

Little Turtle again led some neighboring tribes in an attack on Wayne's troops at Fort Recovery on June 30, 1794. He was repulsed and retreated to the Maumee at the mouth of the Auglaize River. Little Turtle then went on to Detroit to seek British help. The British commander did not dare become embroiled in a war between the Indians and the United States and evaded answering Little Turtle. Thereupon Little Turtle became an advocate for peace, but could not deter the more aggressive Shawnee, Delaware, and Wyandot.

Reinforced by Kentucky militia, Wayne marched to the Maumee on August 8 and began construction of Fort Defiance. A week later he turned down the river to confront the British at their illegal fort. Little Turtle told the Indians that "We have beaten the enemy twice under different commanders . . . The Americans are now led by an officer who never sleeps." He was accused of cowardice and turned over command of the allied Indians to Blue Jacket, a Shawnee war chief.

About three miles above the fort in a tangle of fallen trees, the 1,300 to 1,400 Indians and 50 Canadian rangers gathered to stop Wayne. A rain storm early on August 20 caused a defection among the tribesmen that left only about 900 warriors ready for battle. Wayne fell on them in the Battle of Fallen Timbers. In an hour the defeated Indians retreated to the British fort only to find the gates closed against them. Howling at this betrayal by their "friends," they dispersed in the woods. Wayne camped in front of the fort and exchanged written insults with the commander. He did not attack because he knew negotiations were proceeding in London under John Jay. Instead he returned to finish Fort Defiance and lay waste the cornfields there. Then he moved up river to the Miami capital of Kekionga and built Fort Wayne. He returned to winter quarters at Greeneville.

Simcoe sent this map, which he probably made, to his old commander, Sir Henry Clinton.

NWO-35.
Timothy Pickering, Secretary of War, to Anthony Wayne, Major General, commanding the Army of the United States, Philadelphia, April 15, 1795. Autograph document signed, 10 1/2 x 11 1/2.

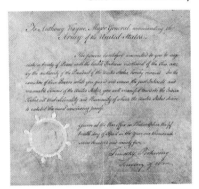

This document is a renewal of "the powers heretofore committed to you to negotiate a treaty of Peace with the hostile Indians northwest of the Ohio," by Pickering, who had just become Secretary of War.

Defeated, and abandoned by their British ally for a second time, the Indian tribes of the Old Northwest saw no alternative to suing for peace with General Wayne. Meanwhile, on November 19, 1794, John Jay's treaty had been signed in London by which, among other things, the British agreed to vacate Fort Niagara, Detroit, Miamis, and Mackinac Island by June 1, 1796, thus removing an irritation to United States sovereignty and an encouragement to Indian hostility.

NWO-36.
"A Treaty of peace, between the United States of America and the tribes of Indians called the Wyandot's, Delaware's, Shawanoe's, Ottawa's, Chipewa's, Putawatime's, Miami's, Eel River Wea's, & Kickapoa's. Greeneville, 9 August 1795. Manuscript copy, 12 p.

General Anthony Wayne convened the first official treaty session on July 15, 1795, and found himself host to 1,130 Indians of ten tribes: in addition to the nine noted above, the Piankeshaw of Vincennes attended and Eel River Wea should have been called Eel River Miami. Little Turtle was the dominant speaker for several of the tribes.

Wayne reminded the chiefs of the treaties made with them since 1783, read them part of the Jay treaty about the British leaving United States soil, and asked for sixteen military reservations on the land retained by the tribes. In reply the Indians first tried to argue that the land belonged to all the tribes in common and could be sold only by unanimous consent. Neither Wayne nor Little Turtle would accept that idea, an old one the British had fostered. Next the Indians asked Wayne to determine the boundaries of the several tribes. He refused this impossible task by saying that each tribe knew its own boundaries better than he. On July 30 he put the question of a peace treaty to a vote, and all the chiefs favored it.

The next four days were devoted to details, including the distribution of medals and ornaments and $20,000 worth of trade goods. In effect the Indians retained only the northwestern part of modern Ohio, where they were to be protected against squatters, and sixteen locations were allotted for trading posts or forts. Annuities of $1,000 to the larger tribes and $500 to the lesser tribes were promised. If the Indians wanted to sell any additional lands, they could sell only to the United States government, but they could continue to hunt on land they had ceded.

Ninety chiefs signed the treaty of Greeneville on August 3, 1796. The copy shown here was written out six days later. The treaty prevented war until 1812.

NWO-37.
Samuel Lewis, *A Map of part of the N: W: Territory of the United States: compiled from actual surveys, and the best information.* Philadelphia, 1796. Outlines in color, 21 1/2 x 30.
Clements Library

This is the clearest map of the Northwest, showing how much of the area had been granted to companies, states, and individuals. A vast amount remained unsurveyed and unavailable for sale to settlers. Lewis (1754?-1822) was a map maker who worked principally in Philadelphia. This map was made for inclusion in an atlas published by Matthew Carey, a Philadelphia printer.

NWO-38.
Rufus Putnam to Oliver Wolcott, Jr., May 18, 1797 and September 18, 1799, Marietta. Two autograph drafts signed, 2 p. each.
Clements Library

The first letter from the Surveyor General of the United States was written to the Secretary of the Treasury announcing that the northern boundary of the military lands west of the surveyed seven ranges was being marked, pursuant to the Treaty of Greeneville. The second letter announced completion of the western boundary agreed upon at the same treaty, from Loramie's Store west to Fort Recovery and south to the Ohio River (anticipated in the preceding Lewis map).

NWO-39.
Augustus Porter, "A Plan of the survey. . . upon the Connecticut-Reserve for the Connecticut Land Company in the year 1796." Manuscript map, 18 x 27.
Clements Library

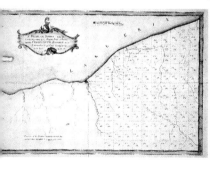

This map of the south side of Lake Erie shows the tract claimed by Connecticut and reserved to that state when western land claims were granted to the federal government. The "fire or sufferers's land" (lower left) was made available to persons in Connecticut who had suffered losses from enemy action during the Revolution. The eastern part of the reserve was surveyed into townships ready for offering to citizens. The map is also the first to show Cleveland, settled in July 1796. Porter was provision contractor to the troops in the Northwest.

NWO-40.
"Plat of that tract of country in the Territory Northwest of the Ohio appropriated for military services, and described in the act of Congress. . ." Manuscript map by Rufus Putnam, 1796, 24 x 36.
Ohio Historical Society

On June 1, 1796, the federal government set aside more than 2,500,000 acres known as the United States Military Tract, between the Ohio Company's grant and that of the Western Reserve, and west of the seven ranges. This tract was to be given to Revolutionary War veterans to fulfill the promise of land bounties for service. Non-commissioned officers and men were to receive 100 acres each, the number increasing for commissioned officers. Putnam ordered this survey of the tract.

NWO-41.
Constitution of the State of Ohio. . .
Chillicothe: From the Press of
N. Willis. 1802. 32 p.

Ohio Historical Society

By act of Congress May 7, 1800, the Northwest Territory was reduced to the area east of a line from the mouth of the Kentucky River to Fort Recovery and thence due north to Canada. The area west of that line was designated Indiana Territory and reverted to the first stage of government with William Henry Harrison as governor and Vincennes as the capital.

The original Northwest Territory was in the second stage of government when Congress approved an enabling act on April 30, 1802, allowing the election of delegates to assemble at Chillicothe and write a constitution for the proposed state of Ohio, its boundaries indicated. Thirty-five delegates were elected November 1, and they assembled and wrote a constitution composed of sections from other state constitutions. It was promptly printed as above.

The legislature was given extensive powers including appointments; it was held in check mainly by frequent elections. The governor was denied a veto. Property qualifications were eliminated for office holders, and the right to vote was extended to all white males who either paid a tax or worked on the roads in their home county. The constitution was approved by Congress on February 10, 1803, and Ohio was admitted to the Union as the seventeenth state, with its present boundaries; the northern part (half of modern Michigan) was added to Indiana Territory.

NWO-42.
James O. Lewis, *Tens-qua-ta-wa or the One that Opens the Door, Shawnee Prophet, Brother of Tecumthe.* Painted at Detroit, 1823. Colored lithograph, 17 x 11.

See illustration on page 38

Clements Library

In the first decade of the nineteenth century, Governor Harrison at Vincennes enjoyed repeated success in persuading the Indians to sell land to the government. He secured the southern third of modern Indiana, almost all of Illinois, and a wedge of southwestern Wisconsin. Then resistance hardened under the leadership of two Shawnee: Tecumseh, a war chief, and his one-eyed brother, Tensquatawa, the Prophet, a religious exhorter. In 1810 Tecumseh grew more threatening and belligerent. The Prophet harangued the tribes to give up the white man's clothes, utensils, tools, liquor, and guns and live like their ancestors, without money or manufactures.

In July 1811 Tecumseh stopped at Vincennes again to warn Harrison. He was on his way south to unite the southern and western tribes. He claimed that all lands were held in common and could not be sold without the consent of all tribes. Harrison decided to act in his absence. With a regiment of regulars and enough militia to comprise a force of about 1,000, he marched up the Wabash in late September. At modern Terre Haute he paused long enough to build a fort, then moved up the river to the mouth of the Tippecanoe tributary, where the Prophet's village was located. Harrison encamped three-quarters of a mile from the village on November 6. Before dawn the Indians attacked Harrison, after The Prophet had performed some magic to insure their success.

The magic failed, the Indians fled, and The Prophet's town was deserted. It was not an easy victory for Harrison, with 62 killed and 126 wounded, but Tecumseh's plans were in ruins. The Indian losses were somewhat less, but faith in The Prophet was shaken. Tecumseh moved closer to the British as the War of 1812 came nearer.

NWO-43.
"View of Cincinnati on the Ohio" in Jervis Cutler, *A Topographical description of the State of Ohio, Indiana Territory, and Louisiana. . .* Boston: Published by Charles Williams. 1812. 219 p.

As the chief commercial center of Ohio, Cincinnati had a population of 2,320 in 1810. It was the trading center for products rafted down the tributary rivers to the Ohio River to the Mississippi River to New Orleans. The town boasted a bank, two printing shops, two wool-carding machines, a cotton factory, twenty-four retail stores, twenty-three taverns, six carriage makers, fifteen brick layers, fifteen masons, twelve weavers, nine blacksmiths, nine lawyers, eight tailors, eight physicians, two brewers, two boat builders, and one jeweler. The stores carried much the same goods that were found in cities east of the Alleghenies.

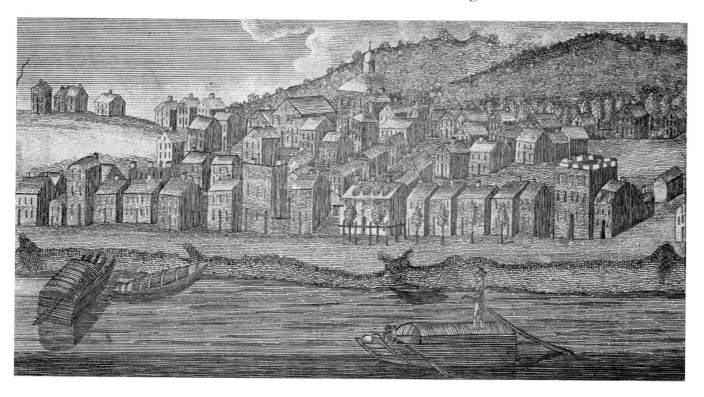

NWO-44.
Quebec Mercury Extraordinary,
August 6, 1812, Montreal.
Broadside, 7 1/4 x 9 1/4.

The War of 1812 began on June 18. The first actions, as related here, were the capture of the Mackinac Island fort before the residents or garrison knew that war had been declared and the advance of Governor William Hull from Detroit into Canada, from which he had retreated a month later. A few days later he surrendered Detroit to a Canadian-Indian force. Hull's surrender included Fort Dearborn (Chicago). Governor Harrison of Indiana Territory resigned to become commander of the second northwestern army.

NWO-45.
Farmer's Watch Tower. vol. I, no. 9, August 26, 1812, Urbana, Ohio. 4 p.

This newspaper, close to the scene of action, is opened to page two reporting the disgraceful surrender of Detroit on August 16, and the massacre of Captain Nathan Heald's garrison at Fort Dearborn (Chicago) after he evacuated the post on August 15 on orders from General Hull. Heald encountered a force of 400 Potatwatomi and ordered an attack on them. After losing twenty-six of fifty-four regulars, all of the twelve militia, two of the nine women, and twelve of the eighteen children, he surrendered to the chief, Black Bird. The surviving prisoners later escaped or were ransomed. The file of this newspaper is unique.

NWO-46.
Richard Dillon, Jr., *Michilimackinac, on Lake Huron.* Montreal: Published by Richard Dillon. 1813. Colored engraving, 11 x 13.

See illustration on page 39

This view of the recently captured fort on Mackinac Island shows the former United States fort on the bluff, a two-masted schooner in the bay, houses of French and British fur traders, and several Indians. In 1815, after stalling as long as possible, the British returned all forts and territory to the United States in accord with the Treaty of Ghent which ended the war.

NWO-47.
Pen and ink sketch of the Detroit River, enclosed in John Hale's letter to Lord William Amherst, Quebec, September 12, 1812. Manuscript map, 18 1/4 x 14 1/2.

Clements Library

Hale writes that he received this map from General Sir Isaac Brock, the victorious commander of Canadian forces. It shows the initial moves of Generals Hull and Brock and the sites of military actions.

NWO-48.
Massacre of the American Prisoners, at French-town, on the River Raisin, by the Savages, under the command of the British General Proctor: January 23rd 1813. Colored engraving, 12 1/4 x 16.

See illustration on page 40

Clements Library

This unique print carries no date or place of publication. It is obviously a contemporary propaganda piece designed to inflame Americans against the British and Indian forces. The artist is unfamiliar with the geography or architecture of the place. Frenchtown is modern Monroe, Michigan, on the River Raisin about thirty-five miles southwest of Detroit.

With a force of 600 men and the same number of Indians, British Colonel Henry Proctor attacked Brigadier General James Winchester at the River Raisin and defeated his force of 1,000 and capturing Winchester himself. Proctor marched off with most of his prisoners, but left approximately eighty wounded ones behind under guard of about fifty Indians. The latter became drunk and murdered several of the prisoners; in the morning they killed a few more. Some of the remaining wounded were taken to a Canadian fort and others were taken to Indian villages. The northwestern army lost more than one hundred killed in battle or at the hands of the Indian guards. The name of Proctor was reviled in America.

NWO-49.
T. Birch, *Perry's Victory on Lake Erie.* Engraved by A. Lawson. 26 x 31.

Clements Library

General William Henry Harrison knew that before he could invade Canada the British fleet on Lake Erie would have to be taken. Captain Oliver Hazard Perry, who commanded the new fleet built on Lake Erie, welcomed the assignment although he lacked full crews to man his ships. His opponent was British Captain Robert Barclay, who also faced a manpower shortage. Moreover, Barclay knew that British troops could not remain in Detroit unless they were regularly provisioned by vessels crossing Lake Erie and ascending the Detroit River.

Perry hovered around Put-in-Bay in western Lake Erie looking for the enemy. On September 10, 1813, Barclay came up with six ships against Perry's eight, but Barclay's vessels carried more guns and of longer range. He preferred to fight at a distance, while Perry wanted to fight at close quarters. Both commanders formed their battle lines with Barclay having the wind at his back. Then the wind shifted to favor Perry. For three hours they shelled each other, until Barclay surrendered. He had lost 41 killed and about 100 wounded; Perry lost 27 killed and about the same number wounded. He sent a famous message to General Harrison: "We have met the enemy and they are ours. . ."

The way was now open for invading Canada and a showdown with the British and their Indian allies under Tecumseh.

NWO-50.
"Treaty of peace and amity between His Britanic Majesty and the United States of America. Done in triplicate at Ghent the twenty fourth day of December 1814." Signed manuscript copy, 13 p.

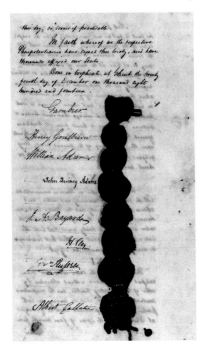

In the Battle of the Thames, October 5, 1814, General Harrison defeated the British under General Proctor, who was retreating eastward from Detroit, and killed the leader of his Indian allies, Tecumseh. While some military leaders in Canada wanted to continue the war, both Great Britain and President Madison sought peace. Delegates had been sent to Ghent, Belgium, where negotiations dragged on for months before they agreed on terms to end the war. So far as it affected the Northwest, the treaty called for mutual restoration of all forts and respect for the boundary lines established in 1783. It did not resolve all the problems that caused the war. In a sense the British sold out the Indians for the third time and enabled the United States to continue getting further cessions to the upper Mississippi and beyond.

The treaty is signed and sealed by Admiral Gambier, Henry Goulburn, and William Adams for the British, and by John Quincy Adams, James Bayard, Henry Clay, Jonathan Russell, and Albert Gallatin for the Americans. It is one of three official copies made, and in the handwriting of Henry Clay, who was helping the clerks get away for Christmas eve. It was retained by Goulburn. The Treaty of Ghent was ratified by the United States Senate on February 17, 1815.

NWO-51.
P. van Huffel, Original pencil sketches of the five American commissioners for the Treaty of Ghent, 1815. 8 x 5.

See illustrations on page 53
Jonathan Russell is not shown.

A few days before the commissioners left Ghent to return home, P. van Huffel, a Dutch artist and president of the Societe des Beaux Arts, asked if he could sketch them in black pencil. They consented. Perhaps he made two sketches of each man, as he kept a set of the five and presented it to Christopher Hughes in March 1817.

John Quincy Adams

Henry Clay

NWO-51

A. Albert Gallatin

James Ashton Bayard

53

NWO-52.
James O. Lewis, *The Aboriginal port-folio: a collection of portraits of the most celebrated chiefs of the North American Indians.* Philadelphia, 1835-1836. Eighty colored plates in ten parts, 17 x 11.

Four portraits of chiefs from the largest tribes inhabitating the Old Northwest are shown here in native dress. They are identified as Miaqua, a Miami chief painted at Mississinews, Indiana, in 1827; Kaanunderwaaguinsem or Berry Picker, a Chippewa chief painted at Prairie du Chien, Wisconsin, in 1825; Menoquet, a Pottowattomie chief, painted at Fort Wayne, Indiana, in 1827; and Cuttaatastia, a Fox chief painted at Prairie du Chien, Wisconsin, in 1825.

James O. Lewis (1799-1858) was employed by the government in 1823 to paint portraits and Indian scenes by attending treaties and other gatherings. Thomas L. McKenney, head of the Bureau of Indian Affairs, intended to build a collection of Indian paintings for the Bureau. By 1834 Lewis was disappointed with the lack of recognition and quit his job in order to publish his own book of eighty colored plates serially. The expense put Lewis in bankruptcy. McKenny and Hall published their illustrated three-volume *History of the Indian Tribes of North America, 1838-44* and used some of Lewis's pictures.

NWO-53.
The Constitution of the State of Indiana, Louisville: Printed by Butler & Wood. 1816. 28 p.

Indiana Territory had passed through the preliminary two stages of government as the population increased. The district next to Ohio and between Lake Michigan and the Ohio River had sufficient population and fifteen organized counties to petition Congress for a constitutional convention. Congress passed an enabling act on April 19, 1816, and set the northern boundary line to include ten miles of Lake Michigan, contrary to the line stipulated in the Ordinance of 1787, so that Indiana might have a port. A convention of forty-three delegates met at Corydon, the territorial capital, on June 10 and in nineteen days framed an excellent constitution that drew heavily on the experience of neighboring states.

It was unusually democratic in extending voting rights and advanced for its time in establishing a system of education "ascending in a regular graduation from township schools to a state university" which the new state could not afford for years. Slavery was immediately prohibited and a bill of rights was listed. The constitution was declared operative on June 29, and state officers were elected. The resolution for admission of Indiana, the nineteenth state, into the Union was approved by President James Madison on December 11, 1816. The remainder of the Northwest Territory was divided between Michigan Territory and Illinois Territory.

NWO-54.
John Melish, *Map of Indiana prepared by John Melish the surveys furnished by Burr Bradley.* Philadelphia, 1817. 19 1/2 x 15 1/2.

Lilly Library

The first map of the state of Indiana, shows its northern boundary pushed ten miles above the line stipulated in the Ordinance of 1787 to make possible a port on Lake Michigan. Above Indiana, Michigan Territory had been set off in 1805 and the remainder of the Old Northwest was called Illinois Territory, since 1809, contrary to what the map indicates.

Settlement of Indiana moved in general from south to north, rather than the traditional flow from east to west.

NWO-55.
The Constitution of the State of Illinois. Kaskaskia: Blackwell & Berry. 1818. 24 p.

Lilly Library

The enabling act passed by Congress on August 18, 1818, authorizing a constitutional convention reduced the population from 60,000 to 40,000 and allowed the northern boundary of the proposed state to be drawn sixty-two miles above the tip of Lake Michigan, as was stipulated in the Ordinance of 1787.

The thirty-three elected delegates met at a local tavern in Kaskaskia on August 3 and after only twenty-one working days shaped a constitution based on those of Ohio, Indiana, Kentucky, and New York. It was made operative at once, without submission to the people, and state officers were elected. On December 3, 1818, the act admitting Illinois to the Union as the twenty-first state was signed by President James Monroe.

Slavery was prohibited, although property rights in slaves and indentured servants resident in the state were recognized. Five years later agitation arose for a convention to amend the constitution. It was understood by the people that the amendment would allow the introduction of slavery. The campaign over the proposal to call the convention lasted eighteen months, then the electorate soundly rejected the idea.

NWO-56.
Fielding Lucas, Jr., *Illinois,* Baltimore, [1823]. Colored map, 15 1/4 x 11 3/4.

Lilly Library

Up to 1825, when the Erie Canal opened, immigration into Illinois came mainly via the Ohio River. The state filled from south to north, although at the Treaty of Greeneville, 1795, the United States obtained a tract of land around Fort Dearborn (Chicago). In 1803 the Kaskaskia sold off the southern tip of the future state. The next year the Sauk and Fox gave up adjoining land farther north. Then the Piankeshaw sold off some land in central Illinois. Discovery of lead mines in northwestern Illinois in the 1820's attracted settlers there even though the area was not safe until after Black Hawk's war.

After nine years as a territory and five years a state, Illinois was almost completely surveyed in 1823, except for the northeastern section, still in Indian hands.

NWO-57.
Fielding Lucas, Jr., *Michigan Ter.*
Baltimore, [1824]. Map, 12 x 15.

This printed map shows Michigan; Wisconsin to the Mississippi River; the Missouri Territory beyond; the northern edges of Illinois; Indiana; and Ohio with its disputed boundary with Michigan resolved in favor of the latter. Various Indian tribes are roughly located. The outlines of the three western Great Lakes are not accurate.

Michigan Territory was created and named in 1805. Its boundaries approximated the present state. The western part of the Northwest Territory was called Indiana Territory. When the state of Indiana was admitted to the Union in 1816, followed by Illinois in 1818, modern Wisconsin and the eastern part of Minnesota were attached to the Michigan Territory, as shown here, until 1835.

NWO-58.
"Walk-in-the-Water with Detroit in the background," attributed to George Washington Whistler. Gouache drawing *c.* 1820, 24 1/4 x 33 1/4.

Whistler (1800-1849) was born at Fort Wayne, where his father was commandant, and he graduated from West Point in 1819. Two years later he taught drawing to the cadets. Walk-in-the-Water, built in 1818, was the first steamship on the western Great Lakes and inaugurated regular service between Buffalo and Detroit. The Indians were convinced it was pulled through the water by a huge sturgeon. She ventured once to Mackinac and to Green Bay, in Lake Michigan. She was wrecked in a storm in 1821, but was succeeded by other steamships. No longer was Detroit cut off from the East in bad sailing weather. Soon the completion of the Erie Canal (1825) would bring thousands of settlers pouring into Ohio, Michigan, and Wisconsin.

NWO-59.
*Constitution of the State of
Michigan. . .* Detroit: Printed by
Sheldon M'Knight. 1835. 20 p.
State Historical Society
of Wisconsin

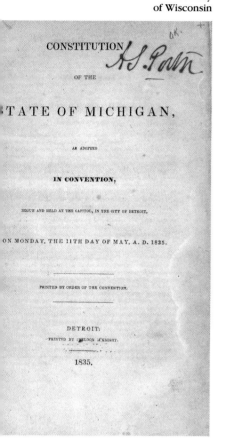

CONSTITUTION

OF THE

STATE OF MICHIGAN,

AS ADOPTED

IN CONVENTION,

BEGUN AND HELD AT THE CAPITOL, IN THE CITY OF DETROIT,

ON MONDAY, THE 11TH DAY OF MAY, A. D. 1835.

PRINTED BY ORDER OF THE CONVENTION.

DETROIT:
PRINTED BY SHELDON M'KNIGHT.

1835.

As usual, this constitution was based largely on those of neighboring states, although it featured a liberal franchise: all white males twenty-one years old or older who resided in Michigan at this time were qualified to vote, including aliens. Also unique was the requirement that a state superintendent of public instruction be appointed. Except for a few top officials, all other state officers and judges were appointed by the governor with the consent of the legislature. The first article listed twenty-one rights of individuals.

This constitution was drafted by ninety-one elected delegates meeting in Detroit on May 11, 1835, for forty-five days. It was submitted to the people on October 5 for ratification, along with the election of state officers prescribed in the document. On November 1 the state legislature convened and state government began, but Michigan was not yet admitted to the Union owing to a boundary dispute with Ohio.

Michigan insisted on a line running east from the tip of Lake Michigan, as stipulated in the Ordinance of 1787, although such a line had been violated in forming Indiana and Illinois. If observed, Michigan would have taken Toledo and a strip of land about eight miles wide. Ohio naturally objected and enlisted the aid of Congressmen from the other two states. As a compromise, President Jackson and a majority of Congress proposed an enabling act that would compensate Michigan for giving up its "Toledo strip" by giving it the eastern upper peninsula—which the people of Michigan considered to have no value.

To approve of this arrangement a new "convention of assent" met at Ann Arbor on September 25, 1836, but delegates rejected the compromise. Reconsideration led to a second convention at Ann Arbor on December 14 and the compromise was accepted. Accordingly President Jackson signed a bill on January 26, 1837, admitting Michigan to the Union as the twenty-sixth state.

NWO-60.
John Farmer, *Improved map of
the territories of Michigan and
Quisconsin. . .* [Detroit?] 1835. 18
x 34 3/4.
Clements Library

This detailed map was outdated almost as soon as it was published. Ohio, Indiana, and Illinois are properly shown as states, and north of them all was Michigan Territory, which encompassed the northern part of the former Northwest Territory. But Michigan had prepared a state constitution in 1835 and applied for admission to the Union (item 59). The application was delayed by her quarrel with Ohio until January 1837. The area west of Lake Michigan extending to the Missouri River was renamed Wisconsin Territory in April 1836. This map was no longer accurate. In 1838 the region west of the Mississippi was separated and called Iowa Territory.

NWO-61.
Constitution of the State of Wisconsin. . . Madison: H. A. Tenney, Printer. 1848. 43 p.

State Historical Society of Wisconsin

The population of the Wisconsin area variously included in Indiana, Illinois, and Michigan territories, exceeded 130,000 by 1840. Yet statehood seemed to be feared because of possible higher taxes and stronger government. A constitution was written in 1846 but rejected by Wisconsin voters because of certain objectionable provisions: prohibition of banks, married women to hold property in their own names, forty-acre homesteads exempted from forced sale for debt, and Negro suffrage.

A second convention of sixty-nine elected delegates met in Madison on December 15, 1847, and after six week's work agreed to this constitution on February 1, 1848. The question of banks was referred to the state legislature, as was any exemption of homesteads from forced sale. The rights of married women to hold property and of Negroes to vote were simply dropped, although the legislature was empowered to extend the suffrage, subject to approval by popular vote. It too contained a declaration of individual rights of twenty-two sections. State debt for internal improvements was forbidden the legislature.

The new constitution was approved by the voters on March 13, 1848. President Polk signed the act admitting Wisconsin, the thirtieth state, to the Union on May 29.

NWO-62.
Edwin Whitefield, *View of St. Anthony, Minneapolis, and St. Anthony falls.* . . New York, 1857. Lithograph, 24 x 26

Minnesota Historical Society

Whitefield (1816-1892) arrived in the United States from Dorset, England, around 1837 and earned his living as an energetic producer of sketches, watercolors, and lithographs. He was an enterprising commercial artist, hopefully putting together views of cities and houses for publication. He spent three years in Minnesota as agent for the Minnesota Land Agency before going to Chicago in 1860, but the union with art was unsuccessful. Even though he never made much money from his pictures, his numerous and accurate views of American cities are historically very valuable. He later enjoyed success in Canada with exhibitions and sales.

NWO-63.
The Constitution of the State of Minnesota . . . Saint Paul: Earle S. Goodrich, State Printer. 1857. 20 p.

State Historical Society
of Wisconsin

CONSTITUTION

OF THE

STATE OF MINNESOTA.

PREAMBLE.

WE, the people of the State of Minnesota, grateful to God for our civil and religious liberty, and desiring to perpetuate its blessings, and secure the same to ourselves and our posterity, do ordain and establish this Constitution :

ARTICLE FIRST—*Bill of Rights.*

SECTION 1. Government is instituted for the security, benefit and protection of the people, in whom all political power is inherent, together with the right to alter, modify, or reform such Government, whenever the public good may require it.

SEC. 2. No member of this State shall be disfranchised, or deprived of any of the rights or privileges secured to any citizen thereof, unless by the law of the land, or the judgment of his peers. There shall be neither slavery nor involuntary servitude in the State, otherwise than in the punishment of crime, whereof the party shall have been duly convicted.

SEC. 3. The Liberty of the press shall forever remain inviolate, and all persons may freely speak, write and publish their sentiments on all subjects, being responsible for the abuse of such right.

SEC. 4. The right of trial by jury shall remain inviolate, and shall extend to all cases at law without regard to the amount in controversy ; but a jury trial may be waived by the parties in all cases, in the manner prescribed by law.

SEC. 5. Excessive bail shall not be required, nor shall excessive fines be imposed ; nor shall cruel or unusual punishments be inflicted.

SEC. 6. In all criminal prosecutions the accused shall enjoy the right to a speedy and public trial, by an impartial jury of the

First settlements appeared in the area between the St. Croix and Mississippi rivers in the 1840's, but after Wisconsin became a state in 1848 an area comprising all of modern Minnesota and most of the Dakotas contained only 4,000 inhabitants. A treaty with the Sioux opened western Minnesota to settlement. Newcomers flooded in by the thousands, including loggers wanting to cut the virgin pine and hardwoods. Territorial status was granted in 1849. By 1852 Minneapolis was laid out next to Fort Snelling, and the population of the territory exceeded 20,000, even though the California gold rush was pulling thousands farther west.

In 1857, when the population approached 150,000, 114 elected delegates assembled at St. Paul on July 13 to draft a constitution. They numbered fifty-five Democrats and fifty-nine members of the new Republican party, both partisan in the extreme. The two parties met separately and wrote two constitutions. Finally, on August 29 a joint committee agreed on a unified constitution, heavily borrowed from older states and containing nothing innovative. It was ratified by the electorate on October 13, when an election of state officials occurred. Admission to the Union became enmeshed in the slavery dispute in Kansas, and not until May 11, 1858, did President James Buchanan sign the act for admission of Minnesota as the thirty-second state. With amendments, this constitution remains the framework of government for the state today.

Robert R. Livingston Esq.

WE the People of the United States, in order to form a more perfect Union, establish Justice, insure domestic Tranquillity, provide for the common Defence, promote the general Welfare, and secure the Blessings of Liberty to ourselves and our Posterity, do ordain and establish this CONSTITUTION for the United States of America.

ARTICLE I.

Sect. 1. ALL legislative powers herein granted, shall be vested in a Congress of the United States, which shall consist of a Senate and House of Representatives.

Sect. 2. The House of Representatives shall be composed of members chosen every second year by the people of the several states, and the electors in each state shall have the qualifications requisite for electors of the most numerous branch of the state legislature.

No person shall be a representative who shall not have attained to the age of twenty-five years, and been seven years a citizen of the United States, and who shall not, when elected, be an inhabitant of that State in which he shall be chosen.

Representatives and direct taxes shall be apportioned among the several states which may be included within this Union, according to their respective numbers, which shall be determined by adding to the whole number of free persons, including those bound to service for a term of years, and excluding Indians not taxed, three-fifths of all other persons. The actual enumeration shall be made within three years after the first meeting of the Congress of the United States, and within every subsequent term of ten years, in such manner as they shall by law direct. The number of representatives shall not exceed one for every thirty thousand, but each state shall have at least one representative; and until such enumeration shall be made, the state of New-Hampshire shall be entitled to chuse three, Massachusetts eight, Rhode-Island and Providence Plantations one, Connecticut five, New-York six, New-Jersey four, Pennsylvania eight, Delaware one, Maryland six, Virginia ten, North-Carolina five, South-Carolina five, and Georgia three.

When vacancies happen in the representation from any state, the Executive authority thereof shall issue writs of election to fill such vacancies.

The House of Representatives shall chuse their Speaker and other officers; and shall have the sole power of impeachment.

Sect. 3. The Senate of the United States shall be composed of two Senators from each state, chosen by the legislature thereof, for six years; and each senator shall have one vote.

A   Immediately

The Philadelphia Convention and The Development of American Government

by Pauline Maier

The Virginians arrived early. Gradually other delegates drifted into Philadelphia, drawn from the far reaches of the United States to take up a work that they knew would be of historic importance. If the constitutional convention of 1787 failed to repair the "defective" governmental systems then in place, James Madison predicted, the people would soon renounce the blessing of self-government and "be ready for any change that may be proposed to them." And if the American republic failed, Roger Sherman said, mankind might well "despair of establishing Governments by Human wisdom and leave it to chance, war and conquest." In short, the constitutional convention would "decide for ever the fate of Republican Government;" on its success or failure depended not just the future of the American people, but "the cause of liberty throughout the world."

What lay behind these fears and hopes? The establishment of republican government—of government in which all power came from the people and none from hereditary right—had made the American Independence movement into a revolutionary cause of worldwide significance. Such governments were considered to be inherently unstable: only kings and nobles could command the sustained obedience of a nation. But by 1776 the Americans, building upon their experience under British rule, concluded that freedom and hereditary rule were incompatible and embarked upon a great experiment. They sought to establish a republican system of government that would both protect freedom and be more durable than the republics of past history. Between 1776 and 1780 all thirteen of the original states either adopted new, written, republican constitutions or adapted their old royal charters in ways that made their people self-governing. Then, in 1781, they ratified Articles of Confederation that formally established a "perpetual Union" of the states. But by 1787 the republican experiment was in trouble.

The difficulty lay in part with the Confederation, which proved too weak to bind the nation together. In 1776 and 1777, when the Articles of Confederation were drafted, Americans were unwilling to grant the confederation those powers to tax and regulate commerce that they had denied Parliament. Subsequent efforts to amend the Articles so Congress could levy duties and pass trade laws failed to receive the required unanimous consent of the states. Congress hoped to alleviate its chronic financial distress by organizing and selling the land it held north of the Ohio River, and continued to work toward that goal even while the federal convention met, passing the Northwest Ordinance in July 1787. However, Congress's control of the Northwest, indeed of all the territory it held between the Appalachians and the Mississippi, remained in doubt. The British refused to give up their posts in the Northwest territory as they had agreed to do in the Treaty of Paris (1783) because, they said, the American states had violated Treaty provisions with regard to Loyalists. About that Congress could do nothing. Nor could Congress stop British efforts to encourage a separatist movement in Vermont, or Spain's attempts to win the allegiance of American settlers in Kentucky and Tennessee. In fact, Congress found it increasingly difficult to gather a quorum of seven state representations so it could do any business at all.

Problems within the states also prompted fears for the republic. Madison thought that the baneful record of the new-formed state governments "contributed more to that uneasiness which produced the Convention, and prepared the public mind for a general reform" than the Confederation's inadequacy. State legislatures passed debtor-relief laws and other measures so unjust "as to alarm the most steadfast friends of Republicanism." Many states also proved unwilling to honor their obligations under the Articles of Confederation. Such sins of commission and omission brought into question "the fundamental principle of republican Government, that the majority who rule in such governments are the safest Guardians both of public Good and private rights." It also made discontent and disorder, the scourge of republics, the order of the day. In past times they had led, almost inevitably, to the establishment of military rule and the annihilation of freedom.

Concern over the fate of the republic, and so of the American Revolution, helped draw a remarkable group of people to Philadelphia in the spring and summer of 1787. Of the fifty-five delegates who attended the federal convention, eight had participated in the constitutional conventions of their states, seven had been governors, and thirty-nine—over seventy percent of the total—had served in the Continental Congress. One of every three had been in the Continental Army, which also increased their commitment to the United States as a nation.

The average delegate was forty-two years old, but the most brilliant of them were even younger. Alexander Hamilton of New York was thirty, James Madison of Virginia—"the father of the Constitution"—thirty-six. James Wilson of Pennsylvania, whose contributions to the convention rivalled Madison's, was eight years older than Madison. He had, however, arrived from his native Scotland only in 1765. As a result, like the younger delegates, he learned the art of American politics under the popular institutions of the Revolution, not the old colonial system. That was important. Such men were not only practicing scientists, fascinated with the challenge of constructing institutions so the American republic could survive longer than any republic in times past; they were experienced politicians who knew how to get things done in a democratic system.

The list of delegates also included several older Americans who brought considerable prestige to the convention, particularly Benjamin Franklin and George Washington, the ex-commander of the Continental Army and the most respected person in the United States. Some notable Americans were absent: John Adams and Thomas Jefferson, for example, were serving their country as diplomats in Europe. Even so, when Jefferson reviewed the convention's membership he characterized it as "an assembly of demigods."

Certainly the distinction of the delegates was out of keeping with the work of a convention "for the sole and express purpose of revising the articles of confederation," as the Continental Congress had described its mission in February 1787. From the beginning, some people questioned whether so august a set of delegates would gather for so limited a task. "I smelt a rat," Patrick Henry explained when asked why he had refused to attend the convention. Later he and other Antifederalists would charge that the convention conspired to undermine the American Revolution by destroying the states and replacing them with a great "consolidated government" like that which the British had tried to establish in the years before 1776.

Henry had cause for suspicion. Many delegates expected to do more than amend the Articles of Confederation; after all, in September 1786 the Annapolis Convention had called for a convention to meet in Philadelphia on the second Monday in May 1787 to "take into consideration the situation of the United States" and "devise such further provisions as shall appear to them necessary to render the constitution of the federal government adequate to the exigencies of the Union." Five months later, when Congress issued its own call for a convention at the same place and time, it similarly spoke of changes that would "render the federal constitution adequate to the exigencies of government, and the preservation of the union." Most delegates agreed that to achieve that objective the central government had to be given substantially more power—more, perhaps, than could be accomplished by revising the Articles of Confederation.

What the Philadelphia convention proposed was, however, not a reincarnation of the British Empire, but what Madison later described as "a new Creation—a real nondescript," namely, American federal system. No delegate had such a system clearly in mind when the convention first assembled in May 1787. It emerged during the convention, which adopted the Virginia Plan as the foundation for its deliberations, then thoroughly revised and expanded that plan in creating the Federal Constitution. Only after the convention dissolved did the Founding Fathers understand what they had accomplished.

Adopting the Virginia Plan

Between May 25 and 29 the convention elected its president, Washington, and secretary, Major William Jackson, and defined its basic rules of proceeding. Each state's delegation would vote as a unit, and seven states would constitute a quorum. (At the time that rule was adopted only nine states were represented, though in the end all the original thirteen states except Rhode Island would participate in the convention.) Moreover, the convention's proceedings were to be secret: the yeas and nays on specific proposals would not be recorded so delegates could more freely change their opinions, and nothing said in the convention was to be communicated to the outside world "without leave." Finally the convention turned to its "main business."

Governor Edmund Randolph of Virginia took the floor. He spoke of the crisis that led to the calling of the convention and "the necessity of preventing the fulfillment of the prophecies of the American downfall," he summarized what was essential in any revised governmental system, and why the Articles of Confederation, though the best that could be achieved eleven years earlier "in the then infancy of the science, of constitutions, and of confederacies," was no longer adequate. Finally, Randolph proposed to replace the Confederation with a new plan of government—the Virginia Plan. It consisted of fifteen resolutions outlining a new national government that would include a bicameral legislature with power to "legislate in all cases to which the separate States are incompetent, or in which the harmony of the United States may be interrupted" by separate state laws. The new legislature would, moreover, be able to "negative," or veto, state laws that in its opinion violated the articles of Union, and to use force against states that failed to fulfill their duties under those articles. The Virginia Plan also provided for a separate "National Executive" and a "National Judiciary." The new scheme of government was to be ratified by special assemblies, constitutional conventions, elected by the people of the various states for that purpose.

Both Randolph's remarks and his proposal showed the influence of Madison, who was perhaps the most knowledgeable student of government among the delegates at Philadelphia. Madison had prepared carefully for the convention by studying the history of all previous confederations in history, their strengths and defects, and examining with equal care the "vices" of American government in the 1780's. From those studies he sought groundrules for the revision of American institutions. His conclusions shaped the Virginia Plan.

The convention rigorously discussed the Virginia Plan from May 30 through June 13, revising and expanding the original Randolph proposals. Meanwhile, more delegates arrived, many of whom were uncomfortable with the direction of change to which the convention had apparently committed itself. Finally, on June 15, William Paterson of New Jersey presented to the convention an alternative plan, one that better represented the views of several "small state" delegates. It became known as the New Jersey Plan.

The Virginia and New Jersey plans differed in their provisions for representation. According to the Virginia Plan, representation in both houses of the national legislature would be proportional to population of contributions to the national treasury. Under the New Jersey plan, each state would continue to be represented equally, as was true in the Confederation's Congress. To delegates from states like Virginia that had relatively large populations, or that expected their populations to grow substantially in the future, the principle of proportional representation had been "improperly violated" in the confederation. The delegates from Delaware, however, said that they were bound by their instructions to consent to no change in the system of equal state representation, and "in case such a change should be fixed on, it might be their duty to retire from the Convention." New Jersey was equally insistent. If the small states would not confederate on a plan of proportional representation, James Wilson responded, Pennsylvania "& he presumed some other states" would confederate on no other. Disagreement over representation, in short, ran deep, and explains in part why the "small state" delegates developed the New Jersey Plan.

The supporters of the New Jersey plan were, however, no less determined than those of the Virginia Plan to enhance significantly the powers of the central government, and so to give it, as David Brearly of New Jersey said, "energy and stability." The New Jersey plan explicitly granted the central government power to raise its own revenue and to regulate commerce, which the central government would also have received under the more general provisions of the Virginia Plan. Although it would have continued the unicameral legislature of the Confederation, the New Jersey Plan authorized the establishment of a separate Executive branch and of a "federal Judiciary" whose members would hold office "during good behavior," such that, in the end, the institutions it proposed would have resembled those of the Virginia Plan. Moreover, all acts of Congress made under the powers vested in it and all treaties ratified under the authority of the United States would be "the supreme law of the respective States," and the federal Executive would have power "to call forth [the] power of the Confederate States. . . to enforce and compel an obedience to such Acts, or an observance of such Treaties" on the part of states *or bodies of men within any state* who interfered with the execution of such laws and treaties.

Supporters of the New Jersey Plan argued that a constitution founded upon the Virginia Plan would have little chance of being ratified. "Our object," Paterson said, "is not such a Government as may be best in itself, but such a one as our Constituents have authorized us to prepare, and as they will approve." As a result, the New Jersey Plan was drafted in a way that made it seem more in keeping with the purpose of the convention as defined by the Continental Congress: it proposed to "revise" as well as to correct and enlarge the Articles of Confederation "to render the federal Constitution adequate to the exigencies of Government, & the preservation of the Union." The government proposed under the New Jersey Plan would therefore have remained "federal" in the language of the day. That is, it would have remained a Confederation of sovereign states (though the New Jersey Plan violated the "federal" nature of the Confederation by providing that the central government could enforce its authority on individuals directly). In proposing the Virginia Plan, Randolph had argued that a union "merely federal" in that sense was insufficient to provide for the "common defense, security of liberty, and general welfare." A "national Government" was necessary, he said, one that would be "supreme." On the same assumption, Alexander Hamilton proposed the establishment of a still more clearly "consolidated" national government. "Two Sovereignties can not co-exist within the same limits," he said, repeating the established wisdom of his time. He would therefore have placed "complete sovereignty in the general Governm[en]t" and reduced the states to administrative units of that new-formed sovereign nation. Hamilton's plan, however, went too far: it was never seriously considered by the convention, no doubt because, as he admitted, it had no chance of being accepted at that time by a people whose attachments to the states remained strong. But did the New Jersey Plan have any better prospect? All previous attempts to increase the Confederation's power by amendments to the Articles of Confederation had failed to get the necessary unanimous state support, and therefore Paterson's plan, George Mason argued, "never could be expected to succeed."

The convention's decision on June 19, by a vote of seven to three, to proceed on the basis of the Virginia Plan was a critical one. It meant that the delegates had agreed to cut loose from the Confederation and follow Washington's advice to adopt "no temporizing expedients," but probe the defects of the current system "to the bottom, and provide a radical cure." They were, however, no more ready than the proponents of the New Jersey Plan to go so far that their proposal would have no chance of ratification. In revising and developing the Virginia Plan, they had to find ways to answer accusations that they "meant to abolish the State Governm[en]ts altogether," to devise a system of government, as Madison later put it, that would "avoid the inefficacy of a mere confederacy without passing into the opposite extreme of a consolidated gov[ernmen]t." In doing that, they provided the foundations for a new definition of the word "federal," one that allowed a genuine sharing of power between two levels of government.

Revising the Virginia Plan

The Virginia Plan was not a complete plan of government. As originally presented, it included blanks for the convention to fill: Randolph's proposals, for example, specified only that members of the first branch of the national legislature "be elected by the people of the several States every _____ for the term of _____; to be of the age of _____ years at least. . . ." Moreover, some provisions in the plan were included mainly to focus debate. They may have represented the best thoughts of the Virginia delegation before the convention met, but even members of that delegation sometimes changed their minds in the course of the convention's debates. Madison, for example, decided soon after the Virginia Plan was presented that the use of force against states would be a mistake because it "would look more like a declaration of war, than an infliction of punishment." In any case, the Virginia Plan was far briefer than a constitution. Clearly it would have to be thoroughly discussed, expanded, reorganized, and rewritten before the convention's work was done.

After its vote of June 19, the convention focused its attention again on the Virginia Plan, which it had already expanded from the original fifteen to nineteen resolutions. By July 26 the convention had agreed upon twenty-three resolutions, many of them longer than any of those originally proposed by Randolph. The convention then recessed until August 6. Meanwhile, a Committee of Detail expanded Congress's resolutions into a draft constitution, which the convention again debated and changed. Finally, on September 8, another committee was appointed "to revise the style of and arrange the articles which had been agreed to by the house." Even after that Committee of Style completed its work, and on through September 17, when the convention finally dissolved, the delegates made further important revisions. The result was a constitution which, though built on the Virginia Plan, was strikingly different from its parent document. Above all, the convention more carefully divided and balanced power among the three branches of the central government, and between the states and the nation.

The most pressing issue before the convention concerned the legislature, the subject of Article I of the Constitution. Dangerous divisions over representation were finally healed on July 16 with the convention's "Great Compromise," which allowed the states equal representation in the Senate. Representation in the House of Representatives would, however, be proportional to the number of free persons, including those bound to service for a term of years and three-fifths "of all other Persons," but excluding "Indians not taxed." Direct taxes were to be apportioned in the same way. Moreover, all money bills were to originate in the lower house, and a census would be taken every ten years so representation and taxation could be allocated appropriately.

The "other persons" mentioned were, of course, slaves. The "three-fifths" rule was taken from a proposed amendment of 1783 to the Articles of Confederation; it was not the result of a separate compromise at the convention. Counting three-fifths of a state's slave population in determining its representation in the House of Representatives served to increase the power of those Southern states whose delegates had argued so strongly for proportional representation in both parts of the legislature. They had done so because they expected the population of the South to grow more rapidly than that of the North. Ironically, that expectation proved wrong: in the early 19th century the Northern population—and so Northern representation in the House of Representatives—rapidly outran that of the South. As a result, the Senate, with the equal representation of states that the Southern delegates so opposed, proved the most important branch of the legislature for the cause of "Southern rights."

How would the legislators be chosen? According to the Virginia Plan, the people would elect the lower house, which would then elect the upper house from candidates nominated by state legislatures. The convention agreed that the House of Representatives should be popularly elected: that, Madison argued, would help establish a "necessary sympathy" between the people and their government. Congressmen's terms were set at two years, but Senators were given six-year terms in the hope that they would bring "due stability and wisdom" to the legislature. The convention gave state legislatures the right to elect Senators, which made the Senate more independent of the House of Representatives than it would have been under the Virginia Plan and so a more effective check upon that body, but tied the Senate more closely to the states. Later, however, the convention decided that Senators would vote individually, not as state units.

Defining the powers of Congress was a task of enormous importance that provoked remarkably little controversy. After some deliberation, the convention abandoned the Virginia Plan's vague statement that Congress could act where the states were "incompetent" or where separate state legislation would interrupt "the harmony of the United States" for a very specific summary of Congress's rights. Much of that summary was simply taken from the Articles of Confederation. Congress was also given critical new powers, starting with the all-important "power to lay and collect taxes" and "to regulate commerce," and the major residual authority "to make all Laws which shall be necessary and proper" for carrying out "all. . . Powers vested by this Constitution in the Government of the United States, or in any Department or Officer thereof." It was denied certain powers—to pass bills of attainder or ex-post facto laws, for example. Prohibitions on the states were more far-reaching. The states were denied the right to "coin Money; emit Bills of Credit; make anything but gold and silver Coin" legal tender, or pass laws "impairing the Obligation of Contracts," all of which they had done in the 1780's, undermining the rights of property and provoking fear for the future of the republic. In the end, the powers of the states were so severly curtailed and those of Congress so enhanced that, Madison noted, the central government would hold "powers far beyond those exercised by the British Parliament, when the States were part of the British Empire."

The convention quickly decided to invest the executive power—Article II of the Constitution—in a single person, despite the objections of Edmund Randolph. Had it thereby created an "elective Monarchy" or, as Wilson argued, a responsible public servant who would be a "safeguard against tyranny"? Unlike a king, the president would be impeachable, and so removable from office for violations of his trust. The convention also set the president's term of office at seven years, after which he could not be re-elected. Gradually, however, the president was given far more than the "general authority to execute the National laws" and the other "Executive rights vested in Congress by the Confederation" that the Virginia Plan mentioned. The president could veto acts of the legislature (though that veto could be over-ridden by a two-thirds vote in Congress), and he could do so by himself, without the "Council of Revision" specified in the Virginia Plan. He would be "Commander in Chief of the Army and Navy of the United States, and of the Militia of the several States." With the advice and consent of the Senate, he could make treaties and appoint ambassadors, judges, and other federal officers. A seven-year term seemed too long for so powerful an executive. In part for that reason, the convention cut it to four years and eliminated the ban on re-election.

The Virginia Plan's provision for letting the legislature elect the president also seemed increasingly unsatisfactory given the convention's inclination to make the president so powerful. Election by Congress would lead to "cabal and corruption." Moreover, as Madison noted, experience in the states "had proved a tendency in our governments to throw all power into the Legislative vortex." State executives were "in general little more than Cyphers: the Legislatures omnipotent." Clearly "the preservation of Republican Gov[ernmen]t. . . required" that the executive provide an "effectual check. . . for restraining the instability and encroachments of the legislature." It seemed unlikely that the executive could be adequately independent of the legislature to provide such a check if it were elected by Congress.

How else could the president be elected? By the people, James Wilson argued; but others said the candidates would be unknown to the people at large. That problem was, Wilson said, "the most difficult of all on which we have had to decide." It was resolved, finally, by entrusting election of the the president to a body of electors equal to the number of senators and representatives states were entitled to send to Congress who would be chosen according to a method defined by their state legislatures. The electors would meet in their states and vote for two persons; Congress would collect and count their ballots. Later, with the development of political parties, presidential electors would be chosen by popular vote rather than by state legislatures, and all of a state's electoral votes would go to that candidate who won a majority of popular votes within the state. The states then became a much more prominent part of presidential elections than the delegates at Philadelphia had expected.

Under the Virginia Plan, the judicial power—Article III of the Constitution—would have consisted of "one or more supreme tribunals" and "inferior tribunals. . . chosen by the National Legislature." Instead the convention called for a single supreme court and "such inferior Courts as the Congress may from time to time ordain and establish." Judges would, moreover, be chosen by the president with the Senate's consent, not by the legislature. In the Constitution, as in the Virginia Plan, the independence of judges would be secured by giving them tenure in office during good behavior, and forbidding the reduction of their salaries while they remained on the bench.

The convention also adopted a critical passage, slightly revised, from the New Jersey Plan, declaring that the Constitution as well as laws and treaties made under its authority were "the supreme Law of the Land" and binding state judges to uphold them, "any Thing in the Constitution or Laws of any State to the Contrary notwithstanding." That, in effect, provided an effective substitute for the Virginia Plan's congressional negative on state laws, which critics had condemned as impractical. There would be, they argued, too many laws for Congress to review, and the proposal "would disgust all the States." "A law that ought to be negatived will be set aside in the Judiciary departm[en]t," Gouverneur Morris said, "and if that security should fail, may be repealed by a Nation[a]l law." Madison remained unconvinced; a congressional veto of state laws still seemed to him "essential to the efficacy and security of the Gen[era]l Gov[ernmen]t." Virginia, Massachusetts, and North Carolina were in the minority when the convention agreed to deny Congress that power.

Most important, the Virginia Plan proposed that the convention's recommendations "be submitted to an assembly or assembled. . . expressly chosen by the people, to consider and decide thereon." The convention agreed, and provided further that when nine state conventions had ratified the Constitution it would go into effect over the people of those states (Article VII). The fate of the Constitution would not therefore be decided by the state legislatures which, as Rufus King noted, lost power under its provisions and so would "be most likely to raise objections." Nor would a single state, or even four states, have power to block the Constitution's establishment. When, moreover, nine states had ratified, the pressure on the others (which were expected to include New York and Virginia) would be intense: they would have to decide not whether they preferred the Articles of Confederation or the Constitution, but whether they would join the new-formed nation or remain apart from it.

Finally, the ratification provisions assured that the new government would be firmly founded upon "the supreme authority of the people themselves." A system of government ratified by the legislatures, Madison argued, could be at best a league or treaty, like the Articles of Confederation; the authority of "a Constitution" had to be "founded on the people." Thus the opening words of the new constitution: "We the people of the United States. . . do ordain and establish this constitution for the United States of America."

A New Form of Government

The convention had accomplished much of what it set out to do. It had divided power between the states and the nation, taking from the states those powers they had abused in the past, and creating a central government with power sufficient to serve the needs of the Union. In designing the new central government, the convention also created independent executive and judicial branches to check the power of the legislature. At each step in its proceedings the convention drew on the lessons of history, including that of the Confederation and the American state constitutions. "Experience must be our only guide," John Dickinson had said; "Reason may mislead us."

But what kind of government had the convention adopted? Not a "federal" government in the sense of a Confederacy, nor a "consolidated" national government. Most delegates agreed on the need for strengthening the central government, and believed they could do that safely. The history of all previous confederacies had proved, Madison claimed, that such governments were endangered more by "anarchy" than "tyranny," by the "disobedience of. . . members" rather than "usurpations of the federal head." The convention was nonetheless forced repeatedly to negotiate compromises between those who thought the states "should be considered as having no existence" with respect to the general government, and those who sought repeated affirmations of the states' continued importance. Even when the delegates agreed to eliminate the word "national" from the Constitution, they did so for different reasons. The result was a system of government that conformed to no previous model and which satisfied no one completely. To Madison and Wilson, for example, the Constitution's provision for equal state representation in the Senate constitutd a new "vice" of the American system, an error of design that would lead to "disease, convulsions, and finally death itself." The Constitution included no reference to a "perpetual Union," as had the Articles of Confederation, perhaps because its future seemed so troubled.

On the final day of the convention, Benjamin Franklin, the convention's only octogenarian, offered his colleagues counsel. "I confess," he said in a speech read for him by James Wilson, "that there are several parts of this Constitution which I do not at present approve, but. . . the older I grow, the more apt I am to doubt my own judgement, and to pay more respect to the judgement of others." A general government, he thought, was necessary for the United States, and he doubted that another convention could devise a better constitution than the one in hand. "Thus I consent. . . to this Constitution because I expect no better, and because I am not sure, that it is not the best. The opinions I have had of its errors, I sacrifice to the public good." He urged the other delegates to do the same, to "doubt a little" of their "own infallibility," and work "heartily and unanimously" for the Constitution's ratification.

Three of the delegates who remained in Philadelphia rejected Franklin's advice—Elbridge Gerry of Massachusetts and two Virginians, Edmund Randolph and George Mason, whose discontent witnessed how far the convention had moved from the original Virginia Plan. However, thirty-nine signed the Constitution and campaigned for its ratification (as, in the end, did Randolph). Their concerted efforts were critical in overcoming the opponents of strong central government, who were far more numerous and powerful in the country than they had been in the convention. With the accession of New Hampshire in June 1787, the necessary nine states had voted to ratify the new Constitution. Within a day a reluctant Virginia added its assent, as did New York, by a close vote (30-27) after long and tortured debates, a month later. In late 1789 North Carolina, and the next year even recalcitrant Rhode Island joined the new government.

In the state ratification debates, moreover, the Federalists, under the leadership of James Wilson, developed a coherent justification of the new American governmental system. Provisions hammered out as compromises emerges as positive virtues. Neither the states nor the central government was "supreme" because in the American Republic the people alone were sovereign. The sovereign people could, moreover, parcel out responsibility for state and national government, creating separate, concurrent jurisdictions over distinct spheres that could "no more clash than two parallel lines can meet," each with complete authority for the tasks delegated to it.

This conception of the state and central governments as independent agencies of the people, separate but equal, provided the intellectual foundation for modern American federalism, a system of government which, as Madison understood, had no historical precedent and so was a "new Creation."

After 200 years, it is tempting to celebrate the Federalists' accomplishments as if they were the end of the story. With justice, it should also be remembered that the conclusions Madison and his colleagues drew from past history in the 1780's were brought into question by the experience of the 1790's: eleven years after the convention "the father of the Constitution" had come to fear tyranny from the central government far more than anarchy, and proposed, in the Virginia Resolutions of 1798, a role for the states in judging the constitutionality of Congress's laws. The struggle to find within a republican constitutional order ways to reconcile majority rule with minority rights, and to achieve at once stability and freedom, continued to concern the generations of Clay and Calhoun and of Lincoln and Douglas.

In the end, the future of the republic was determined less at Philadelphia than at Appomattox, by a great war fought for much the same reason as that for which the constitutional convention met—to assure that "government of the people, by the people, for the people, shall not perish from the earth." The Constitution's longevity is therefore due less to the political and intellectual brilliance of the Founding Fathers than of their willingness, and that of later Americans, to sacrifice their private preferences—to "doubt a little" of their "infallibility"—and work for the success of a government that was, in the way of human creations, imperfect, but the best they were likely to get.

Pauline Maier, a native of Minnesota and a magna cum laude graduate of Radcliffe College, earned her Ph.D. in American history at Harvard University. She has taught at the University of Massachusetts, and since 1978 is professor of history and head of the history faculty at Massachusetts Institute of Technology. She has received several honors and awards, written for scholarly journals, and is the author of *From Resistance to Revolution: Colonial Radicals and the Development of American Opposition to Britain. 1765-1776* (1972) and *The Old Revolutionaries: Political Lives in the Age of Samuel Adams* (1980). This essay has been adapted from an article in the summer 1987 issue of *This Constitution*, and is used with the permission of Project '87, sponsored by the American Historical Association and the American Political Science Association.

Recommended Reading: Nothing written about the constitutional convention is as fascinating as the debates themselves. *Notes of Debates in the Federal Convention of 1787 Reported by James Madison,* with an introduction by Adrienne Koch (Athens, Ohio: Ohio University Press, 1966), which runs to some 660 pages, will serve most readers' needs, but the most dedicated will prefer the first two volumes of *The Records of the Federal Convention of 1787,* edited by Max Farrand (New Haven: Yale University Press, 1911; Yale pb.), which includes the official record and notes on debates taken by Madison and several other delegates, all arranged by date. (The third volume of that set includes appendices, and a fourth, published in 1937, includes corrections in earlier volumes, the first 21 amendments to the Constitution, and a general index.) Max Farrand's *The Framing of the Constitution of the United States* (New Haven: Yale University Press, 1913; Yale pb.), remains a splendid, straightforward account of the convention. That story was told in a more artful way by Carl Van Doren in *The Great Rehearsal: The Story of the Making and Ratifying of the Constitution of the United States* (New York: Viking, 1948; Penguin pb.), Catherine Drinker Bowen in *Miracle at Philadelphia: The Story of the Constitutional Convention, May to September, 1787* (Boston: Little, Brown, 1966), and, more recently, by James L. and Christopher Collier in *Decision in Philadelphia: The Constitutional Convention of 1787* (New York: Random House, 1986).

On the ratification debates, again, nothing compares to Jonathan Elliot, ed., *The Debates in the Several State Conventions on the Adoption of the Federal Constitution,* 5 Volumes (orig. Washington [for Congress], 1854; 2nd ed. Philadelphia: J. P. Lippincott, 1859, 1861, 1863. . .). The Virginia debates in the second volume are especially fascinating. *The Federalist Papers* are always worth reading, and a reliable edition edited by Clinton Rossiter is available in paperback (New York: Mentor Books, 1961). Less well known are the writings of the Constitution's opponents: see Cecelia Kenyon, *The Antifederalists* (Indianapolis: Bobbs-Merrill, 1966), which includes an introduction and several Antifederalists writings, and/or Kenyon's earlier and very influential essay, "Men of Little Faith: The Anti-Federalists on the Nature of Representative Government," *The William and Mary Quarterly,* 3d Series, Vol. X11 (1955), pp. 3-43.

The fullest discussion of the development of American constitutionalism in the Revolutionary era is in Gordon S. Wood's *The Creation of the American Republic, 1766-1787* (Chapel Hill: University of North Carolina Press, 1969; Norton pb.). Though Wood's book has had an enormous impact on contemporary scholarship, not all it says is generally accepted: see the retrospective discussions of the book in *The William and Mary Quarterly,* 3d Series, Vol. XLIV (1987), July 1987. Among the briefer discussions of the Constitutional Convention, the Founding Fathers, and the divisions over ratification see especially Stanley Elkins and Eric McKitrick, "The Founding Fathers: Young Men of the Revolution," *The Political Science Quarterly,* LXXVI (1961), pp. 181-216; John Roche, "The Founding Fathers: A Reform Caucus in Action," *The American Political Science Review,* LV (1961), pp. 799-816, and the final chapter of Pauline Maier, *The Old Revolutionaries: Political Lives in the Age of Samuel Adams* (New York: Knopf, 1980; Vintage pb. 1982), which discusses the divisions of 1787-88 within the larger context of the American Revolution. The first two of these essays, or abridgments of them, are available in several collections, including Leonard W. Levy, ed., *Essays on the Making of The Constitution* (New York: Oxford University Press, 1969; Oxford pb.)

The United States Constitution

The books, pamphlets, broadsides, newspapers, and manuscripts selected for exhibition and described in the following pages mark the bicentennial of the Constitution of the United States. They begin with the origin and minutes of the Philadelphia convention, the working drafts of the Constitution, the opinions of delegates, the proceedings for and against ratification by the states, the election of the first President and Vice-President, to the actions of the first session of Congress in adopting the first ten amendments. The value and importance of these items is unquestioned.

It is obligatory for all citizens to have some knowledge of this remarkable document, for the Constitution is the guarantee of our personal liberties and security, as well as the basis of our national political life. An incomparable legacy from the past, it has provided a stable and flexible government based solely on elections for two hundred years. While it is impossible to recreate historical events of the distant past with indisputable exactitude, the items presented here do much to explain the motives, attitudes, desires, and thoughts of the men who participated in the dramatic events leading up to the framing and implementing of our Constitution.

The Lilly Library materials in this display were acquired primarily from the benefactions of the Ball Brothers Foundation of Muncie and of Richard O. Morris of Indianapolis.

Cecil K. Byrd
Professor and Librarian Emeritus
Indiana University
Bloomington

federal Constitution adequate to the exigencies of
Government, and the preservation of the Union. —

Chw Thoms ousry

By

The United States in Congress Assembled. —

February 21st 1787 —

Whereas there is provision in the Articles of Confederation and perpetual Union for making alterations therein
by the assent of a Congress of the United States, and of the
Legislatures of the several States; And whereas experience
hath evinced that there are defects in the present Confederation, as a mean to remedy which several of the States
and particularly the State of New York by express instructions
to their Delegates in Congress, have suggested a Convention
for the purposes expressed in the following Resolution, and
such Convention appearing to be the most probable mean
of establishing in these States a firm national government

Resolved That in the opinion of Congress it is expedient
that on the second monday in May next a Convention of
Delegates who shall have been appointed by the several
States be held at Philadelphia for the sole and express
purpose of revising the Articles of Confederation, and report-
-ing to Congress, and the several Legislatures, such
alterations and provisions therein as shall when agreed
to in Congress, and confirmed by the States, render the

federal

USC-2

USC-59

USC-1.
"Address of the convention held at Annapolis, in September 1786." Signed at end: "John Dickinson, Chairman. Annapolis, Sept. 14, 1786." In *The American Museum,* vol. I, no. IV, April 1787, pp. 291-4.

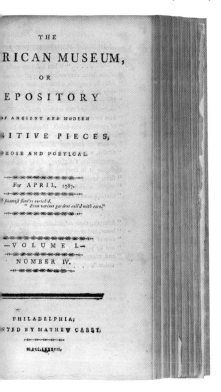

On the initiative of Virginia, the thirteen states were invited to send delegates to discuss interstate commerce at Annapolis, Maryland, in September 1786. Nine states elected delegates, but only those from New York, New Jersey, Pennsylvania, Delaware and Virginia attended. They adjourned after agreeing to call a convention to meet in Philadelphia the next May "to take into consideration the situation of the united states, to devise such further provisions as shall appear to them necessary to render the constitution of the federal government adequate to the exigencies of the union."

The Confederation Congress, then meeting in New York City, considered the Annapolis report and on February 21, 1787, passed its own call, stipulating the meeting was "for the sole and express purpose of revising the Articles of Confederation," under which the present government functioned. All previous attempts to amend the Articles to give Congress power to tax and to regulate trade had failed.

USC-2.
"By the United States in Congress assembled. February 21st 1787. Whereas there is provision in the Articles of Confederation and perpetual Union for making alterations therein. . . Resolved that in the opinion of Congress it is expedient that on the second Monday in May next a Convention of Delegates who shall have been appointed by the several states be held at Philadelphia for the sole express purpose of revising the Articles of Confederation. . . Chas. Thomson secry."
Autograph document signed, 2 p.
See illustration on page 75

This is a manuscript copy of the act passed by the Confederation Congress on February 21, 1787, calling on the states to send delegates to the convention in Philadelphia May 14. Charles Thomson, secretary to Congress, sent copies of the act to all the states the day it was adopted. It also was widely printed in newspapers, appearing in at least thirty-nine between February 24 and March 21, 1787.

USC-3.
[John Quincy Adams, ed.]
Journal, acts and proceedings of the convention, assembled at Philadelphia, Monday, May 14, and dissolved Monday, September 17, 1787, which formed the Constitution of the United States.
Boston: printed and published by Thomas B. Wait. 1819. 510 p.
Richard O. Morris collection, Lilly Library

This is the first printing of the journal kept by William Jackson, secretary to the convention. The *Journal* and a few other documents are the only official surviving papers from the Constitutional convention. Upon adjournment, Jackson was instructed to deposit his papers as secretary with the president of the convention, George Washington. He did so only "after burning all the loose scraps of papers which belong to the Convention." In 1796 Washington deposited the papers with the Department of State. In 1818 a joint resolution of Congress ordered them published.

John Quincy Adams, then Secretary of State, reported that the *Journal* was "no better than the daily minutes from which the regular journal ought to have been, but never was, made out." With assistance from Charles Pinckney and James Madison and with documents from the papers of David Brearly, delegate from New Jersey, the task was completed. This first publication to break the veil of secrecy under which the delegates labored contained no debates.

USC-4.
Robert Yates, *Secret proceedings and debates of the convention assembled at Philadelphia, in the year 1787, for the purpose of forming the Constitution of the United States of America. From the notes taken by the late Robert Yates, esq. Chief Justice of New-York, and copied by John Lansing, Jun. esq. late Chancellor of that state, members of that convention. Including "the genuine information," laid before the legislature of Maryland by Luther Martin, esq. then Attorney General of the state, and member of the same Convention. Also, other historical documents relative to the federal compact of the North American Union.*
Albany: printed by Websters and Skinners. 1821. 308 p.
Richard O. Morris collection, Lilly Library

Yates and Lansing were delegates to the convention from the state of New York. They left Philadelphia on July 10 to attend sessions of the New York Supreme Court (Yates a judge, and Lansing a practicing attorney), and did not return. As they explained in a letter to Governor Clinton written on December 21, 1787, they contended that the proceedings in the convention were violating their instructions as delegates from the state.

Yates' brief, but informative notes, about the attitude of individuals in the debates shed further light on the proceedings.

Luther Martin's *The Genuine Information* was first printed in installments in the Baltimore *Maryland Gazette* beginning December 28, 1787 (item 29). It ends on page 94 of *Secret Proceedings*. Yates' notes begin on page 95 and end on page 207. The remainder of the book contains a variety of reprinted matter relating to the Constitution.

USC-5.

James Madison, *The Papers of James Madison, purchased by order of Congress; being his correspondence and reports of debates during the Congress of the Confederation and his reports of debates in the Federal Convention; now published from the original manuscripts deposited in the Department of State, by direction of the joint library committee of congress under the superintendence of Henry D. Gilpin.* Washington: Langtree E. O'Sullivan. 1840. 3 vols.

Richard O. Morris collection, Lilly Library

James Madison, delegate from Virginia, with a deep sense of history, took voluminous notes on the proceedings in the convention. His report constitutes the fullest and most indispensable source on the drafting of the Constitution. While not a verbatim transcription, it represents a fairly full account of the daily deliberations of the convention.

Madison made some changes in his manuscript subsequent to the convention. He copied the original manuscript of the official *Journal* kept by Secretary Jackson (item 3), borrowed from Washington with whom it had been deposited. Using this he made a number of additions and corrections to his manuscript probably in 1791. He also used Yates's *Secret Proceedings* (item 4) to make a few insertions.

Madison decided on posthumous publication. He died in 1836. Congress purchased his manuscripts for $30,000, and in 1840 the above three volumes were published.

USC-6.

Alexander Hamilton, "Proposition of Col. Hamilton of New York in the Convention for establishing a Constitution of government for the United States." Manuscript document, [1787?]. 3 p.

Lilly Library

This manuscript, presumed to be contemporary from an unknown hand, contains eleven suggestions delivered by Hamilton in a speech to the convention on June 18, 1787. A firm proponent of a strong central government, he advocated an extreme system whereby senators and the chief executive would serve during good behavior; governors of the states would be appointed by the national government; and all state laws would be subordinate to national laws.

Hamilton did not offer his plan as a formal proposal, so it was not referred to a committee or debated. One delegate remarked: "Though he has been praised by everybody, he has been supported by none." Hamilton left the convention for business affairs on June 29, returned between August 6-11, went back to New York soon after August 13, and returned to the convention between September 1-6.

USC-7.

We, the people of the States of New-Hampshire, Massachusetts, Rhode-Island and Providence Plantations, Connecticut, New-York, New-Jersey, Pennsylvania, Delaware, Maryland, Virginia, North-Carolina, South-Carolina, and Georgia, do ordain, declare, and establish the following Constitution for the government of ourselves and our posterity. [Philadelphia: Dunlap and Claypoole. 1787]. Caption title, 7 leaves, printed on one side, numbered [1]-7.

Lilly Library

This is the first printed draft of the Constitution, one of perhaps sixty copies distributed to convention delegates on August 6, 1787. This copy belonged to Pierce Butler, the Irish-born delegate from South Carolina.

On July 24, the convention elected a committee of detail, composed of John Rutledge, Edmund Randolph, James Wilson, Oliver Ellsworth and Nathaniel Gorman, "for the purpose of reporting a Constitution conformably to the Proceeding aforesaid." The convention recessed on July 26, to give the committee of detail time for its assigned task, and met again on August 6.

Edmund Randolph, John Rutledge and James Wilson wrote and annotated several drafts. They exceeded previous resolutions of the convention by including provisions from the Articles of Confederation, material from some of the state constitutions, and plans submitted but not accepted by the convention. The committee then had their final version set in type, corrected the proof sheets, and had some sixty copies printed for the convention membership.

The Constitution as it unfolded in this first printed draft was altered significantly by the convention before agreement in its final form. The preamble was restated from "We the People" of the thirteen states to read "We the People of the United States." The authority of the Senate to make treaties, appoint ambassadors and supreme court judges was vested with the President "by and with the Advice and Consent of the Senate." The election of the President "by the Legislature" for a seven-year term and "not to be elected for a second time" was altered to a four-year term (silent on the number of terms) with election by electors representing the states. As finally agreed upon by the convention the finished document was reduced to seven articles containing twenty-one sections.

USC-8.

We the People of the United States, in order to form a more perfect Union. . . do ordain and establish this Constitution for the United States of America. . . [New York: J. M'Lean. 1787]. Caption title, 4 p.

See illustration on page 82

Lilly Library

Of the several September 1787 printings of the Constitution this one appears, historically, to be one of the most important. The text, with accompanying documents, was the fourth version printed by John McLean, probably done on September 29. It is also the one sent to the thirteen states by the Confederation Congress requesting that it "be submitted to a convention of delegates chosen in each state by the people thereof in conformity to the resolves of the Convention. . ." for ratification or rejection. Note that it was not to be submitted to a state legislature.

The Constitution was to take effect after ratification by nine of the thirteen states.

WE the People of the States of New-Hampſhire, Maſſachuſetts, Rhode-Iſland and Providence Plantations, Connecticut, New-York, New-Jerſey, Pennſylvania, Delaware, Maryland, Virginia, North-Carolina, South-Carolina, and Georgia, do ordain, declare and eſtabliſh the following Conſtitution for the Government of Ourſelves and our Poſterity.

ARTICLE I.

The ſtile of this Government ſhall be, " The United States of America."

II.

The Government ſhall conſiſt of ſupreme legiſlative, executive and judicial powers.

III.

The legiſlative power ſhall be veſted in a Congreſs, to conſiſt of two ſeparate and diſtinct bodies of men, a Houſe of Repreſentatives, and a Senate; each of which ſhall, in all caſes, have a negative on the other. The Legiſlature ſhall meet on the firſt Monday in December in every year.

IV.

Sect. 1. The Members of the Houſe of Repreſentatives ſhall be choſen every ſecond year, by the people of the ſeveral States comprehended within this Union. The qualifications of the electors ſhall be the ſame, from time to time, as thoſe of the electors in the ſeveral States, of the moſt numerous branch of their own legiſlatures.

Sect. 2. Every Member of the Houſe of Repreſentatives ſhall be of the age of twenty-five years at leaſt; ſhall have been a citizen in the United States for at leaſt three years before his election; and ſhall be, at the time of his election, a reſident of the State in which he ſhall be choſen.

Sect. 3. The Houſe of Repreſentatives ſhall, at its firſt formation, and until the number of citizens and inhabitants ſhall be taken in the manner herein after deſcribed, conſiſt of ſixty-five Members, of whom three ſhall be choſen in New-Hampſhire, eight in Maſſachuſetts, one in Rhode-Iſland and Providence Plantations, five in Connecticut, ſix in New-York, four in New-Jerſey, eight in Pennſylvania, one in Delaware, ſix in Maryland, ten in Virginia, five in North-Carolina, five in South-Carolina, and three in Georgia.

Sect. 4. As the proportions of numbers in the different States will alter from time to time; as ſome of the States may hereafter be divided; as others may be enlarged by addition of territory; as two or more States may be united; as new States will be erected within the limits of the United States, the Legiſlature ſhall, in each of theſe caſes, regulate the number of repreſentatives by the number of inhabitants, according to the proviſions herein after made, at the rate of one for every forty thouſand.

Sect. 5. All bills for raiſing or appropriating money, and for fixing the ſalaries of the officers of government, ſhall originate in the Houſe of Repreſentatives, and ſhall not be altered or amended by the Senate. No money ſhall be drawn from the public Treaſury, but in purſuance of appropriations that ſhall originate in the Houſe of Repreſentatives.

Sect. 6. The Houſe of Repreſentatives ſhall have the ſole power of impeachment. It ſhall chooſe its Speaker and other officers.

Sect. 7. Vacancies in the Houſe of Repreſentatives ſhall be ſupplied by writs of election from the executive authority of the State, in the repreſentation from which they ſhall happen. V.

WE the People of the United States, in order to form a more perfect Union, establish Justice, insure domestic Tranquility, provide for the common Defence, promote the general Welfare, and secure the Blessings of Liberty to ourselves and our Posterity, do ordain and establish this CONSTITUTION for the United States of America.

ARTICLE I.

Sect. 1. ALL legislative powers herein granted shall be vested in a Congress of the United States, which shall consist of a Senate and House of Representatives.

Sect. 2. The House of Representatives shall be composed of members chosen every second year by the people of the several states, and the electors in each state shall have the qualifications requisite for electors of the most numerous branch of the state legislature.

No person shall be a representative who shall not have attained to the age of twenty-five years, and been seven years a citizen of the United States, and who shall not, when elected, be an inhabitant of that state in which he shall be chosen.

Representatives and direct taxes shall be apportioned among the several states which may be included within this Union, according to their respective numbers, which shall be determined by adding to the whole number of free persons, including those bound to service for a term of years, and excluding Indians not taxed, three-fifths of all other persons. The actual enumeration shall be made within three years after the first meeting of the Congress of the United states, and within every subsequent term of ten years, in such manner as they shall by law direct. The number of representatives shall not exceed one for every thirty thousand, but each state shall have at least one representative; and until such enumeration shall be made, the state of New-Hampshire shall be entitled to chuse three, Massachusetts eight, Rhode-Island and Providence Plantations one, Connecticut five, New-York six, New-Jersey four, Pennsylvania eight, Delaware one, Maryland six, Virginia ten, North-Carolina five, South-Carolina five, and Georgia three.

When vacancies happen in the representation from any state, the Executive authority thereof shall issue writs of election to fill such vacancies.

The House of Representatives shall chuse their Speaker and other officers; and shall have the sole power of impeachment.

Sect. 3. The Senate of the United States shall be composed of two senators from each state, chosen by the legislature thereof, for six years; and each senator shall have one vote.

Immediately after they shall be assembled in consequence of the first election, they shall be divided as equally as may be into three classes. The seats of the senators of the first class shall be vacated at the expiration of the second year, of the second class at the expiration of the fourth year, and of the third class at the expiration of the sixth year, so that one-third may be chosen every second year; and if vacancies happen by resignation, or otherwise, during the recess of the legislature of any state, the Executive thereof may make temporary appointments until the next meeting of the legislature, which shall then fill such vacancies.

No person shall be a senator who shall not have attained to the age of thirty years, and been nine years a citizen of the United States, and who shall not, when elected, be an inhabitant of that state for which he shall be chosen.

The Vice-President of the United States shall be President of the senate, but shall have no vote, unless they be equally divided.

The Senate shall chuse their other officers, and also a President *pro tempore*, in the absence of the Vice-President, or when he shall exercise the office of President of the United States.

The Senate shall have the sole power to try all impeachments. When sitting for that purpose, they shall be on oath or affirmation. When the President of the United States is tried, the Chief Justice shall preside: And no person shall be convicted without the concurrence of two-thirds of the members present.

Judgment in cases of impeachment shall not extend further than to removal from office, and disqualification to hold and enjoy any office of honor, trust or profit under the United States; but the party convicted shall nevertheless be liable and subject to indictment, trial, judgment and punishment, according to law.

Sect. 4. The times, places and manner of holding elections for senators and representatives, shall be prescribed in each state by the legislature thereof: but the Congress may at any time by law make or alter such regulations, except as to the places of chusing Senators.

The Congress shall assemble at least once in every year, and such meeting shall be on the first Monday in December, unless they shall by law appoint a different day.

Sect. 5. Each house shall be the judge of the elections, returns and qualifications of its own members, and a majority of each shall constitute a quorum to do business; but a smaller number may adjourn from day to day, and may be authorised to compel the attendance of absent members, in such manner, and under such penalties as each house may provide.

Each house may determine the rules of its proceedings, punish its members for disorderly behaviour, and, with the concurrence of two-thirds, expel a member.

Each house shall keep a journal of its proceedings, and from time to time publish the same, excepting such parts as may in their judgment require secrecy; and the yeas and nays of the members of either house on any question shall, at the desire of one-fifth of those present, be entered on the journal.

Neither house, during the session of Congress, shall without the consent of the other, adjourn for more than three days, nor to any other place than that in which the two houses shall be sitting.

Sect. 6. The senators and representatives shall receive a compensation for their services, to be ascertained by law, and paid out of the treasury of the United States. They shall in all cases, except treason, felony and breach of the peace, be privileged from arrest during their attendance at the session of their respective houses, and in going to and returning from the same; and for any speech or debate in either house, they shall not be questioned in any other place.

No senator or representative shall, during the time for which he was elected, be appointed to any civil office under the authority of the United States, which shall have been created, or the emoluments whereof shall have been encreased during such time; and no person holding any office under the United States, shall be a member of either house during his continuance in office.

Sect. 7. All bills for raising revenue shall originate in the house of representatives; but the senate may propose or concur with amendments as on other bills.

Every bill which shall have passed the house of representatives and the senate, shall, before it become a law, be presented to the president of the United States; if he approve he shall sign it, but if not he shall return it, with his objections to that house in which it shall have originated, who shall enter the objections at large on their journal, and proceed to reconsider it. If after such reconsideration two-thirds of that house shall agree to pass the bill, it shall be sent, together with the objections, to the other house, by which it shall likewise be reconsidered, and if approved by two-thirds of that house, it shall become a law. But in all such cases the votes of both houses shall be determined by yeas and nays, and the names of the persons voting for and against the bill shall be entered on the journal of each house respectively. If any bill shall not be returned by the President within ten days (Sundays excepted) after it shall have been presented to him, the same shall be a law, in like manner as if he had signed it, unless the Congress by their adjournment prevent its return, in which case it shall not be a law.

Every order, resolution, or vote to which the concurrence of the Senate and House of Representatives may be necessary (except on a question of adjournment) shall be presented to the President of the United States; and before the same shall take effect, shall be approved by him, or, being disapproved by him, shall be re-passed by two-thirds of the Senate and House of Representatives, according to the rules and limitations prescribed in the case of a bill.

Sect. 8.

USC-9.
The Pennsylvania Packet, and Daily Advertiser, Wednesday, September 19, 1787, Philadelphia. 4 p.

Richard O. Morris collection, Lilly Library

The first public release of the text of the Constitution occurred when it was read to the Pennsylvania Assembly and a large crowd in the gallery on September 18, 1787. The next morning the Constitution was published in five Philadelphia newspapers. The text appearing in *The Pennsylvania Packet* is perhaps the most accurate. Within two months the Constitution was published in at least seventy-five newspapers from Portland, Maine, south to Savannah, Georgia, and west to Lexington, Kentucky. The great mass of people were informed of it through newspapers. The Constitution was available to the public in other forms, for it was extensively published in magazines, broadsides, and books.

Through the tens of thousands of copies that came from the printing presses, and in hundreds of public discussions, the people received the message from the convention at Philadelphia that "We, the People of the United States" could make a new start in self-government by ratifying this Constitution they had forged.

USC-10.
Charles Pinckney, *Observations on the plan of government submitted to the Federal Convention, in Philadelphia, on the 28th of May, 1787. By Mr. Charles Pinckney, delegate from the state of South-Carolina. Delivered at different times in the course of their discussions.* New-York: Printed by Francis Childs. [1787]. 27 p.

Lilly Library

Charles Pinckney advocated a strong central government. According to the official *Journal,* he submitted his plan to the convention on May 29. It was not discussed but turned over to the committee of detail on July 24. His original plan is not known to exist, but from other sources it appeared to contain thirty-one or thirty-two provisions and resembled in many details the Virginia plan submitted by Edmund Randolph.

It may never be known why Pinckney had this pamphlet printed. He declared it was for the information of his friends. Both Washington and Madison thought it was a self-serving gesture. Pinckney thought highly of his own talents and perhaps wanted his contemporaries and posterity to think he played a greater role in the framing of the Constitution than he actually did. Material differences exist in what he proposed in the convention and what he wrote in *Observations.* The pamphlet was reprinted, in whole or in part, in at least seven newspapers.

USC-11.
[Noah Webster.] *An Examination into the leading principles of the Federal Constitution proposed by the late Convention held at Philadelphia. With answers to the principal objections that have been raised against the system. By a citizen of America.* Philadelphia: printed and sold by Prichard & Hall. M.DCC.LXXXVII. 55 p.

Richard O. Morris collection, Lilly Library

Webster, lexicographer, journalist, and pamphleteer, defended the two-house Congress, discussed the powers of the proposed central government as they related to the powers of state governments, and attempted to answer nine objections of the Antifederalists to the Constitution. The pamphlet was published on October 17, 1787. It circulated widely and long extracts appeared in newspapers of Connecticut and Massachusetts.

USC-12.
George Washington to David
Stuart. Mount Vernon 30
November 1787. Autograph letter
signed, 3 p.

Clements Library

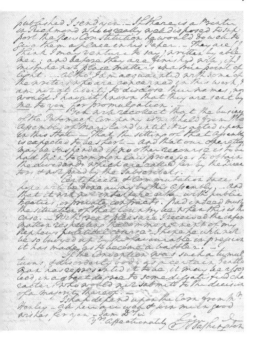

David Stuart, friend and neighbor of Washington, was an Alexandria physician. He represented Fairfax County in the Virginia House of Delegates and was a delegate to the Virginia ratifying convention, where he voted to ratify the Constitution.

Washington's letter is devoted to the literature then circulating concerning the Constitution. "I have seen no publication yet, that ought, in my judgement, to shake the proposed Government in the mind of the impartial public." He sent Stuart the first seven numbers of *The Federalist,* stating: "If there is a Printer in Richmond who is really well disposed to support the New Constitution he would do well to give them a place in his paper. They are (I think I may venture to say) written by able men. . ."

USC-13.
Samuel A. Otis to Elbridge
Gerry. New York, 2d Jany 1788.
Autograph letter signed, 4 p.

Lilly Library

Otis of Boston represented Massachusetts in the Confederation Congress in 1787 and 1788. Gerry, also of Massachusetts, served in the Continental Congress, signed the Declaration of Independence, and was a delegate to the Constitutional convention, but refused to sign the completed Constitution and opposed its ratification. Otis differed with him politically but was friendly. He expressed the hope that Massachusetts would discuss the ratification question "with that decorum & dignity of debate which have marked her public Councils. . ."

The completed Constitution was delivered on September 20, to the Confederation Congress, which could only debate it because special state conventions were called for to vote acceptance or rejection of the document. Proponents came to be called Federalists, and those opposed, Antifederalists. The strongest argument of the latter was the absence of a bill of rights, as guaranteed in some state constitutions. The Federalists were better organized and were supported by most of the ninety-five or so newspapers in the thirteen states. Decisions on ratification are reported in the following exhibits.

USC-14.

The Pennsylvania Packet, and Daily Advertiser. Monday, December 10, 1787, Philadelphia. 4 p.

Richard O. Morris collection,
Lilly Library

This newspaper announced the first ratification of the Constitution by the state of Delaware. Thirty delegates, elected on November 26, met at Dover, December 7-11, and unanimously voted for adoption of the Constitution. There are no records of debates in the convention, but the wording of the form of ratification would indicate general acceptance:

> We the Deputies of the People of the Delaware State, in Convention met. . . Have approved of, assented to, ratified, and confirmed, and by these Presents, DO, in virtue of the Power and authority to us given for that purpose, for, and in behalf of ourselves and our constituents, fully, freely, and entirely approve of assent to, and ratify and confirm the said CONSTITUTION.

News of Delaware's prompt action spread rapidly throughout the country via newspapers.

USC-15.

[Tench Coxe,] *An Examination of the Constitution for the United States of America, submitted to the people by the general convention, at Philadelphia, the 17th day of September, 1787, and since adopted and ratified by the conventions of eleven states, chosen for the purpose of considering it, being all that have yet decided on the subject. By an American citizen. To which is added, a speech of the Honorable James Wilson, esquire, on the same subject.* Philadelphia: printed by Zachariah Poulson. MDCCLXXXVIII. 33 p.

Richard O. Morris collection,
Lilly Library

Coxe, the Philadelphia-born political economist, merchant, land speculator, and public servant, was most active in support of the Constitution during the ratification period. *An Examination* consists of four letters by Coxe on the subject of the Constitution, designed to counter Antifederalist opposition, particularly in the back country of Pennsylvania, prior to the state convention. The four letters were the first major defense of the Constitution to be published. The first three appeared in the *Independent Gazeteer* (Philadelphia) September 26, 28, and 29, 1787; the fourth appeared on October 24.

The speech of James Wilson, Scotland-born lawyer, political theorist, Congressman, land speculator, and one who played a major role in drafting the Constitution, occupies pages 25 to 33 with the caption title: *Substance of an address to a meeting of the citizens of Philadelphia: delivered, October sixth. . .* Wilson spoke for ratification, attempting to refute Antifederalist arguments that were beginning to circulate concerning the nature of the proposed Constitution. He declared in a grand predictive finale that "It is the BEST FORM OF GOVERNMENT WHICH HAS EVER BEEN OFFERED TO THE WORLD." Wilson's speech became the Federalist interpretation of the Constitution nationwide.

USC-16.
Proceedings and debates of the General Assembly of Pennsylvania. Taken in short-hand by Thomas Lloyd. Volume the first. Philadelphia: printed by Daniel Humphreys. M,DCC,LXXXVII. 143 p.

Lilly Library

The volume covers the debates in the Assembly from September 4 through 29, 1787. Thomas Lloyd, London-born, had settled in Philadelphia where be became a professional shorthand writer and teacher. The above volume is the first of four which he published, on four sessions of the Pennsylvania Assembly, September 4, 1787 to October 4, 1788. The first two volumes contain the debates over the calling of the state convention to consider the Constitution.

Pennsylvania was the first state to call a convention to consider the Constitution, and the second state to ratify. Her actions attracted national attention, and the act of ratification gave momentum to that movement nationwide. Ratification was accomplished by strong-arm action of the General Assembly and a highly organized propaganda campaign conducted by supporters of the Constitution. The vote did not reveal the widespread opposition to the Constitution in the state.

An actively organized two-party system existed in Pennsylvania at the time the Constitution was framed. The General Assembly was in session when the Constitutional convention adjourned. A strong nationalist group which controlled the Assembly was determined to call a state convention to consider ratification before adjournment and succeeded.

USC-17.
"The Address and Reasons of Dissent of the Minority of the Convention of the State of Pennsylvania to their Constituents." *The Pennsylvania Packet, and Daily Advertiser,* December 18, 1787, Philadelphia. 4 p.

Richard O. Morris collection, Lilly Library

This "Dissent," signed by twenty-one of twenty-three members who voted against ratification in the Pennsylvania state convention, summarizes the arguments against the Constitution and includes fifteen amendments proposed at the convention but not recorded. "Dissent" served as a model for resisters in states yet to consider the Constitution.

USC-18.
Verfabren der Vereinigten Convention, gehalten zu Philadelphia, in dem Jahr 1787, und dem Zwolften Jahr der Americanischen Unabhangigkeit. Germantown: Gedruckt bey Michael Billmeyer [1787]. 16 p.

Lilly Library

The Pennsylvania Assembly, on September 24, 1787, directed that 2,000 copies of the Constitution be printed in English and 1,000 copies in German for distribution throughout the state. The printer, Michael Billmeyer, was the publisher of *Die Germantauner Zeitung,* a biweekly which supported the Federalist cause.

The German language edition of the Constitution was a concession to the German population of the state, an estimated one-third of the state's population at that time. They represented a powerful force in state politics. Those who were delegates to the state convention were not a cohesive group, some voting to ratify the Constitution and others voting against it.

USC-19.
Anthony Wayne, Manuscript notes taken at the Pennsylvania ratification Convention. [November 1787]. 4 p.

Anthony Wayne papers, Clements Library

The Pennsylvania-born veteran of the Revolution was a delegate to the state convention representing Chester County. Wayne, who represented the county in the Assembly in 1784 and 1785, participated in the debates infrequently, but spoke for and voted for ratification.

These notes are dated "Tuesday 27th Novemb 1787" and "Friday 30th." On the right of the sheet the speaker and the topic under discussion are sometimes identified. The notes on the left appear to be for Wayne's use.

USC-20.
Debates of the Convention, of the state of Pennsylvania, on the Constitution proposed for the government of the United States. In two volumes. Taken accurately in short-hand, by Thomas Lloyd. Philadelphia: Printed by Joseph James. A.D. M.DCC.LXXXVIII. 147, [3] 150 p.

Lilly Library

Only one of the projected two volumes supporting the Constitution was published. It contains the major speeches of James Wilson in the convention and two short speeches of Thomas McKean.

Tench Coxe distributed printed pages before the volume was published. He wrote James Madison that he was sending sixty pages "which I am anxious to get into the hands of Mr. [Rufus] King for the use of the gentleman in the Massachusetts Convention."

USC-21.
The Constitution, proposed for the government of the United States of America, by the Foederal Convention, held at Philadelphia, in the year one thousand seven hundred and eight-seven. To which is annexed, the ratification thereof by the delegates of Pennsylvania in the state Convention. Philadelphia: Hall and Sellers. M.DCC.LXXXVII. 24 p.

Clements Library

After an energetic, statewide campaign to elect delegates to a state convention, sixty-nine were elected, and two to one they were Federalist. The convention was in session twenty-two days and approved the Constitution on December 12, 1787, by a vote of forty-six to twenty-three, the second state to ratify. On December 15 the convention ordered that the Constitution and ratification notice be printed: 3,000 copies in English and 2,000 in German. No copy of the German language edition is known to exist.

USC-22.
The Pennsylvania Packet, and Daily Advertiser, December 29, 1787, Philadelphia. 4 p.

Richard O. Morris collection, Lilly Library

A news item announced that New Jersey unanimously had ratified the Constitution on December 18, 1787, the third state to do so. There was no organized or open resistance in the state against ratification. New Jersey consistently had supported the movement to give more power to the Confederate Congress. The proposed Constitution gave the state what it desired in national government: a Congress with power to regulate trade, collect taxes, and pay off the national debt.

After the state Assembly had adopted resolutions for a state convention late in October, thirty-nine delegates were elected. They assembled at Trenton in the Blazing Star Tavern on December 11, and in a week voted unanimously to ratify.

USC-23.
Pennsylvania Gazette. February 13, 1788. 4 p.

Clements Library

Georgia was the first Southern state to ratify the Constitution, the fourth state chronologically to give its assent. Most historians agree that the danger from Indians, depreciated currency, and sluggish commercial affairs were factors in the state's decision. Georgia citizens had less to fear from a strong national government than from their current ills.

The Georgia Assembly, on October 26, 1787, called for a state convention to meet in Augusta "to adopt or reject any part or the whole" of the Constitution. The convention was organized on December 28 and the next day considered the constitution paragraph by paragraph, then adjourned. On Monday, December 31, the convention reassembled, and the Constitution was unanimously ratified. Although thirty-three delegates had been elected, no more than twenty-six attended any session. Their decision was welcomed in Pennsylvania and announced in this newspaper.

Connecticut became the first New England state to call for a convention to consider the Constitution. The nine weekly newspapers then published in the state were pro-Federalist and favored ratification. By October 2, the Constitution had been printed in seven of the newspapers, including *The Connecticut Courant* shown here. Roger Sherman and Oliver Ellsworth, two of the state's delegates to the Constitutional convention, reported by letter to Governor Samuel Huntington on September 26, 1787, after their return from Philadelphia. The letter was submitted to the General Assembly. On October 16 the House and Council concurred in resolutions calling for town meetings to elect delegates to meet in convention at Hartford on January 3, 1788. They convened at the State House, then moved to the First Church where the public was permitted to sit in the gallery.

A total of 174 delegates had been elected at town meetings, but only 168 voted, others being absent or ill. On January 9, they voted 128 to 40 to ratify, the fifth state to do so.

USC-24.
The Connecticut Courant, and Weekly Intelligencer, Monday, October 1, 1787, Hartford. 4 p.

Lilly Library

USC-25.

Debates, resolutions and other proceedings, of the Convention of the Commonwealth of Massachusetts, convened at Boston, on the 9th of January 1788, and continued until the 7th of February following, for the purpose of assenting to and ratifying the Constitution recommended by the Grand Federal Convention. Together with the yeas and nays on the decision of the grand question. To which the Federal Constitution is prefixed. Boston: printed and sold by Adams and Nourse, and Benjamin Russell, and Edmund Freeman. M,DCC,LXXXVIII. 219 p.

Richard O. Morris collection,
Lilly Library

DEBATES,
RESOLUTIONS AND OTHER PROCEEDINGS,
OF THE
CONVENTION
OF THE
COMMONWEALTH OF MASSACHUSETTS,

Convened at Boston, on the 9th of *January*, 1788, and continued until the 7th of *February* following, for the purpose of assenting to and ratifying the CONSTITUTION recommended by the Grand FEDERAL CONVENTION.

TOGETHER WITH

The YEAS AND NAYS ON THE DECISION OF THE GRAND QUESTION.

TO WHICH

THE FEDERAL CONSTITUTION

IS PREFIXED.

BOSTON:

Printed and sold by ADAMS and NOURSE, in Court-Street; and BENJAMIN RUSSELL, and EDMUND FREEMAN, in State-Street.

M,DCC,LXXXVIII.

These *Debates* were recorded by printers representing the *Massachusetts Centinel* and *Independent Chronicle* in Boston and were reprinted from them. A later edition (1856) included the official journal and notes on the debates kept by Theophilus Parsons, a delegate to the state convention and later chief justice of the Massachusetts Supreme Court.

The ratification process in Massachusetts was viewed with anxiety by supporters of the Constitution throughout the nation. Massachusetts was a key state, and it was thought that actions there might determine the ultimate fate of the Constitution. The struggle was hard, bitter, and characterized by wild rumor and allegations of corrupt behavior.

Elections for delegates to the state convention were held between November 19, 1787 and January 7, 1788. The towns and districts were entitled to the same number of delegates as they had representatives in the General Court: 364, most of them uninstructed. There was no hall in Boston with adequate seating capacity, so they met in a meeting house. By public subscription stairs were built and seats provided for several hundred spectators, and even a press gallery was added. The convention met from January 9 to February 7, 1788. The Federalist strategy was to ratify the Constitution first and then consider amendments to it.

Governor John Hancock, elected president of the convention, was selected to make the proposal, but he was confined to his bed with gout. Nevertheless, he appeared dramatically before the convention swaddled in flannels, proposed amendments as if they were his own, and assured the delegates they would be enacted speedily once the Constitution was ratified. Opposition crumbled. On February 6 the Constitution was endorsed by the narrow vote of 187 to 168. Massachusetts became the sixth state to ratify.

Analysis of the votes recorded reveals that the sea-coast counties, with strong commercial interest, supported the Constitution with 102 votes for, and 19 against. Non-coastal counties voted 60 for and 128 against. Counties in the future state of Maine voted 25 for ratification, 21 against. The nine amendments recommended to be added to the Constitution were largely written by Theophilus Parsons. Massachusetts was the first state to propose amendments along with ratification, setting a pattern for the states that followed. All except Maryland and Rhode Island were to ratify and simultaneously propose amendments.

USC-26.
[Mercy Otis Warren,]
Observations on the new Constitution and on the foederal and state conventions. By a Columbian patriot. Boston printed, New-York reprinted. M,DCC,LXXX,VIII. 22 p.

Richard O. Morris collection, Lilly Library

Mrs. Warren, historian, poet, and dramatist, strongly opposed ratification of the Constitution. She criticized the "partizans of monarchy" and accused the Federalists of "fraudulent designs." The pamphlet was first published in February 1788, soon after Massachusetts had acted. It was reprinted in New York and widely circulated in that state.

She was familiar with both the Constitution and the literature that circulated during the period of ratification. She described some eighteen objections to the document, which included most of the amendments. Above all, Mrs. Warren feared that the Constitution, which she called "this many-headed monster," would destroy state government.

USC-27.
The Constitution or frame of government, for the United States of America. [Printed by Thomas and John Fleet, in Boston. 1788]. Caption title. 23 p.

See illustration on page 94

Lilly Library

This pamphlet contains the Constitution and documents forwarding it to the states, the resolution of the General Court of Massachusetts calling the state convention, the form of ratification, and the amendments proposed by the state. The pamphlet is open to show the recommended amendments, three of which were adopted subsequently in the national Bill of Rights.

USC-28.
[Alexander Contee Hanson,]
Remarks on the proposed plan of a Federal government, addressed to the citizens of the United States of America, and particularly to the people of Maryland, by Aristides. Annapolis: printed by Frederick Green, printer to the state [1788]. 42 p.

Clements Library

Hanson, judge of the Maryland General Court, 1778-89, and state chancellor, 1789-1806, was a delegate to the state convention from the city of Annapolis. He voted to ratify. This pamphlet of his appeared on January 31, 1788, well before delegates to the state convention were elected in April. Seventy-six delegates were elected, two of whom did not attend because of illness, and twelve of whom were committed Antifederalists. The convention met at Annapolis April 21-29. After debate the delegates voted to ratify 63 to 11, making Maryland the seventh state to join the Union.

The people of Maryland had ample time to ponder the Constitution. Antifederalists were quoted in newspapers. Hanson's pamphlet defended the provisions for the legislative and executive branches of the proposed government and argued that a bill of rights was unnecessary. He maintained that Maryland under the Constitution would no longer be a "poor member of a defenseless system of petty republics." Washington wrote letters to Marylanders warning that if the state rejected the Constitution, it would be defeated in Virginia.

USC-29.
Luther Martin, *The Genuine information delivered to the legislature of the state of Maryland, relative to the proceedings of the general Convention, lately held at Philadelphia: by Luther Martin, esquire, attorney general of Maryland, and one of the delegates in the said Constitution. Together with a letter to the hon. Thomas C. Deye, speaker of the House of Delegates, an address to the citizens of the United States, and some remarks relative to a standing army, and a bill of rights.* Philadelphia: printed by Eleazer Oswald. M,DCC,LXXXVIII. VIII, 93 p.

Richard O. Morris collection,
Lilly Library

Martin, attorney general of Maryland, was one of the state's delegates to the Constitutional convention and a leading lawyer of the time. He participated frequently in the debates in Philadelphia, wanting a stronger central government without decreasing the power of the states. He was a vigorous opponent of a strong executive and a large standing army, and he thought a bill of rights should be prefixed to the Constitution. He was absent when the Philadelphia convention adjourned and did not sign the Constitution.

This Antifederalist pamphlet is an enlarged and rearranged version of his report to the Maryland house on November 29, 1787. It was first published in the Baltimore *Maryland Gazette* in twelve installments between December 28, 1787, and February 8, 1788. The newspaper installments were widely reprinted in the press of five other states. The pamphlet appeared in early April.

THE

GENUINE INFORMATION,

DELIVERED TO THE

LEGISLATURE of the STATE of

MARYLAND,

RELATIVE TO THE PROCEEDINGS

OF THE

GENERAL CONVENTION,

LATELY HELD AT PHILADELPHIA;

BY

LUTHER MARTIN, ESQUIRE,

ATTORNEY-GENERAL OF MARYLAND,

AND

One of the DELEGATES in the said CONVENTION.

TOGETHER WITH

A LETTER to the Hon. THOMAS C. DEYE,
Speaker of the *House* of *Delegates*,

An ADDRESS to the CITIZENS of the UNITED
STATES,

And some REMARKS relative to a STANDING
ARMY, and a BILL of RIGHTS.

Nullius addictus jurare in Verba Magistri.——HOR.

PHILADELPHIA;
PRINTED by ELEAZER OSWALD, at the COFFEE-HOUSE.
M,DCC,LXXXVIII.

USC-30.
Constitution of the United States of America, as proposed by the Federal Convention. Charleston: Printed by Bowen, Vandle & Andrews [1788]. Broadside, 19 3/4 x 24.

Richard O. Morris collection, Lilly Library

This is a copy of the Constitution made available to delegates in May 1788 in the South Carolina convention to consider ratification. The main objections to the Constitution had surfaced in the House of Representatives back in January, during discussion over even calling a state convention. Opposition came mainly from back-country legislators, who represented 80% of the state's white population but held only 87 of 231 seats in the legislature. The Charleston area was resented for its wealth and aristocracy and feared for its strong advocacy of the Constitution.

Elections for the state convention were held in April, and 236 delegates were named, although fourteen did not attend. A Federalist majority was chosen. News of ratification in Maryland was a blow to Antifederalist hopes. On May 23 the delegates voted 149 to 73 to ratify the Constitution. Eight states now favored it. As a sop to the opposition, recommended amendments were accepted by the convention.

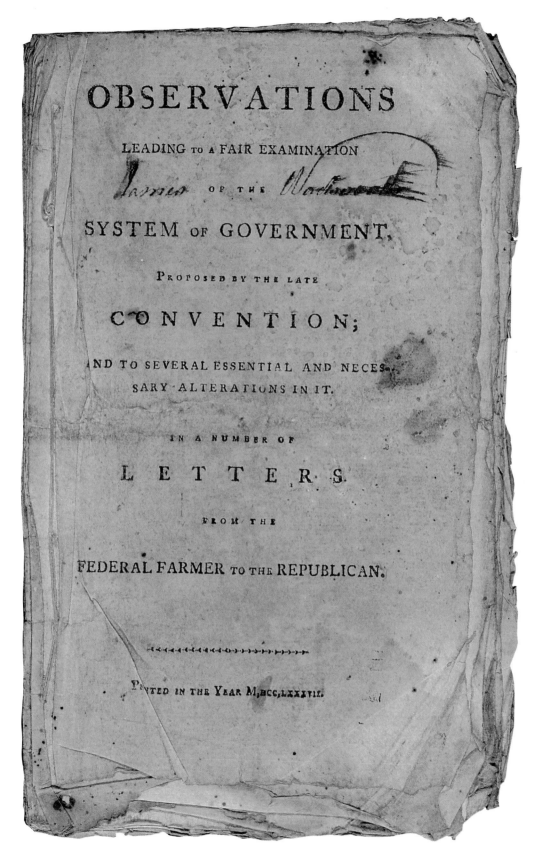

OBSERVATIONS

LEADING to a FAIR EXAMINATION

[handwritten inscription]

OF THE

SYSTEM of GOVERNMENT,

PROPOSED BY THE LATE

CONVENTION;

AND TO SEVERAL ESSENTIAL AND NECES-
SARY ALTERATIONS IN IT.

IN A NUMBER OF

LETTERS

FROM THE

FEDERAL FARMER to the REPUBLICAN.

PRINTED IN THE YEAR M,DCC,LXXXVII.

Government, the Convention do therefore Recommend, that the following Alterations and Provisions be introduced into the said Constitution :

First. That it be explicitly declared that all powers not expressly delegated by the aforesaid constitution, are reserved to the several states, to be by them exercised.

Secondly. That there shall be one Representative to every thirty thousand persons, according to the census mentioned in the constitution, until the whole number of the representatives amounts to two hundred.

Thirdly. That Congress do not exercise the powers vested in them by the fourth section of the first article, but in cases when a state, neglect or refuse to make regulations therein mentioned, or shall make regulations subversive of the rights of the people, to a free and equal representation in Congress, agreeably to the constitution.

Fourthly. That Congress do not lay direct taxes, but when the monies arising from the impost and excise are insufficient for the public exigencies; nor then, until Congress shall have first made a requisition upon the states, to assess, levy and pay their respective proportions of such requisition, agreeably to the the census fixed in the said constitution, in such way and manner as the legislature of the state shall think best, and in such case, if any state shall neglect or refuse to pay its proportion, pursuant to such requisition, then Congress may assess and levy such state's proportion, together with interest thereon, at the rate of six per centum per annum, from the time of payment prescribed in such requisition.

Fifthly. That Congress erect no company of merchants with exclusive advantages of Commerce.

Sixthly. That no Person shall be tried for any crime by which he may incur an infamous punishment, or loss of Life, until he be first indicted by a grand Jury, except in such cases as may arise in the government and regulation of the land and naval Forces.

Seventhly. The supreme judicial federal Court shall have no jurisdiction of causes between citizens of different states, unless the matter in dispute, whether it concerns the reality

or

or personality, be of the value of three thousand dollars at the least : Nor shall the federal judicial powers extend to any actions between citizens of different states where the matter in dispute, whether it concerns the reality or personality, is not of the value of fifteen hundred Dollars, at the least.

Eighthly. In civil actions, between citizens of different states, every issue of fact, arising in actions at common law, shall be tried by a jury, if the parties, or either of them, request it.

Ninthly. Congress shall, at no time, consent, that any person, holding an office of trust or profit, under the United States, shall accept of a title of nobility, or any other title or office, from any king, prince, or foreign state.

And the Convention do, in the name and in behalf of the people of this commonwealth, enjoin it upon their representatives in Congress, at all times, until the alterations and provisions aforesaid have been considered, agreeably to the fifth article of the said constitution, to exert all their influence, and use all reasonable and legal methods to obtain a ratification of the said alterations and provisions in such manner as is provided in the said article.

And that the United States in Congress assembled may have due notice of the assent and ratification of the said constitution by this Convention—It is RESOLVED, That the assent and ratification aforesaid be engrossed on parchment, together with the recommendation and injunction aforesaid, and with this resolution ; and that his Excellency JOHN HANCOCK, Esquire, President, and the Honorable WILLIAM CUSHING, Esquire, vice-President of this Convention, transmit the same, countersigned by the Secretary of the Convention, under their hands and seals, to the United States in Congress assembled.

(Signed) JOHN HANCOCK, President.

WILLIAM CUSHING, Vice-President.

(Countersigned)
GEORGE RICHARDS MINOT, Secretary.

Printed by THOMAS and JOHN FLEET, in *Boston.*

NEW-YORK, May 1.

YESTERDAY took place, according to the resolution of the two houses of Congress, the ceremony of the introduction of his Excellency GEORGE WASHINGTON, to the Presidency of the United States.

The scene was extremely solemn and impressive; we imagine the public cannot be more satisfactorily-informed than by an unembellished recital of the events, and a simple picture of the figures which composed it.

At nine o'clock A. M. the clergy of different denominations assembled their congregations in their respective places of worship, and offered up prayers for the safety of the president.

About twelve o'clock the procession moved from the house of the President in Cherry-street, through Dock-street, and Broad-street, to Federal Hall; in the following order:

Col. Lewis, supported by two officers,
Capt. Stakes, with the troop of Horse,
Artillery,
Major Van Horne,
Grenadiers, under Capt. Harsin,
German Grenadiers, under Capt. Scriba,
Major Bicker,
The Infantry of the Brigade,
Major Chrystie,
Sheriff,
The Committee of the Senate,

The PRESIDENT and suite,

The Committee of the Representatives,
The Hon. Mr. Jay, General Knox, Chancellor Livingston, and several other gentlemen of distinction.

Then followed a multitude of citizens.

When they came within a short distance of the hall, the troop formed a line on both sides of the way, and his Excellency passing through the ranks, was conducted into the building, and in the Senate Chamber introduced to both houses of Congress—immediately afterwards, accompanied by the two houses, he went into the gallery fronting Broad Street, where, in the presence of an immense concourse of citizens, he took the oath prescribed by the constitution, which was administered to him by the Hon. R. R. Livingston, Esq; Chancellor of the state of New-York.

Immediately after he had taken the oath, the Chancellor proclaimed him President of the United States. —Was answered by the discharge of 13 guns, and by loud repeated shouts; on this the President bowed to the people, and the air again rang with their acclamations. His Excellency with the two Houses, then retired to the Senate Chamber where he made the following SPEECH.

Fellow Citizens of the Senate, and of the House of Representatives.

Among the vicissitudes incident to life, no event could have filled me with greater anxieties, than that of which the notification was transmitted by your order, and received on the 14th day of the present month.— On the one hand, I was summoned by my country, whose voice I can never hear but with veneration and

[...] from a retreat which I had chosen with the fondest predeliction, and in my flattering hopes, with an immutable decision, as the asylum of my declining years; a retreat which was every day rendered more necessary as well as more dear to me, by the addition of habit to inclination, and of frequent interruptions in my health to the gradual waste committed on it by [...]—On the other hand, the magnitude and difficulty of the trust to which the voice of my country called me, being sufficient to awaken [...] [...] of his fellow citizens, a diffident scrutiny into his qualifications, could not but overwhelm with despondence, one, who, inheriting inferior endowments from nature, and unpracticed in the duties of civil administration, ought to be peculiarly conscious of his own deficiencies. In this conflict of emotions, all I dare aver, is, that it has been my faithful study to collect my duty from a just appreciation of every circumstance, by which it may be effected. All I dare hope, is, that if in executing this task, I have been too much swayed by a grateful remembrance of former instances, or by an affectionate sensibility to this transcendant proof of the confidence of my fellow citizens; and have thence too little consulted my incapacity as well as disinclination, for the weighty and untried cares before me; my error will be palliated by the motives which misled me, and its consequences be judged by my country, with some share of the partiality in which they originated.

Such being the impressions under which I have in obedience to the public summons, repaired to the present station; it would be peculiarly improper to omit in this first official act, my fervent supplications to that Almighty Being who rules over the universe—who presides in the councils of nations—and whose providential aids can supply every human defect, that his benediction may consecrate to the liberties and happiness of the people of the United States, a government instituted by themselves for these essential purposes; and may enable every instrument employed in its administration, to execute with success, the functions allotted to his charge. In tendering this homage to the great Author of every public and private good, I assure myself that expresses your sentiments not less than my own; nor those of my fellow citizens at large, less than either. No people can be bound to acknowledge and adore the invisible hand, which conducts the affairs of men more than the people of the United States. Every step by which they have advanced to the character of an independent nation, seems to have been distinguished by some token of providential agency. And in the important revolution just accomplished in the system of their united government, the tranquil deliberations, and voluntary consent of so many distinct communities, from which the event has resulted, cannot be compared with the means by which most governments have been established, without some return of pious gratitude along with an humble anticipation of the future blessings which the past seem to presage. These reflexions arising out of the present crisis, have forced themselves too strongly on my mind to be suppressed. You will join with me, I trust, in thinking, that there are none under the influence of which, the proceedings of a new and free government can more auspiciously commence.

By the article establishing the executive department

(left margin, vertical): Civil officers on each side

(right margin, vertical): civil officers on each side

At the General Affembly of the Governor and Company of the State of *Rhode-Ifland* and *Providence-Plantations*, begun and held by Adjournment at *Newport*, within and for the State aforefaid, in Confequence of Warrants iffued by his Excellency the Governor, on *Monday* the Seventh Day of *June*, in the Year of our Lord One Thoufand Seven Hundred and Ninety, and in the Fourteenth Year of Independence.

P R E S E N T,

His Excellency

ARTHUR FENNER, Efquire,

GOVERNOR.

The Honourable

Samuel J. Potter, Efq; Deputy-Governor.

Thomas G. Hazard, Efq;
Peleg Arnold, Efq;
James Arnold, Efq;
Caleb Gardner, Efq;
John Cooke, Efq;
James Congdon, Efq; } Affiftants.
Thomas Hoxsie, Efq;
Thomas Holden, Efq;
Job Watson, Efq;
John Harris, Efq;

Henry Sherburne, Efq; Deputy-Secretary.

DEPUTIES

USC-31.
Members of the Convention, viz.
[Charleston, 1788]. Broadside,
19 1/8 x 15 1/2

This broadside contains the names and parishes represented by the delegates elected to the South Carolina convention which ratified the Constitution. The copy belonged to an unidentified delegate to the convention, who wrote on the verso of the sheet: "Members of the Convention of So. Carolina for the Ratification of the Federal Constitution May 12th 1788." The broadside contains the names of 263 delegates. The unknown delegate wrote in the left margin: "N.B. Those names marked thus √ were in favour of the ratifications those marked + against it." The delegate was attentive, for on May 26 he correctly recorded the vote—149 for, 73 against.

The names of those delegates lined through or not marked as voting represented the absent members, with the exception of Governor Thomas Pinckney. He was the presiding officer, present but not voting.

USC-32.
The Constitution of the United States, as recommended to Congress the 17th of September, 1787. By the Federal Convention. Portsmouth, New Hampshire: printed by John Melcher. 1787. 16 p.

The New Hampshire legislature, in its special session of December 1787, authorized the printing of 400 copies of the Constitution for distribution to town meetings before election of delegates to a state convention. Between December 31 and February 12, 1788, a total of 113 delegates were chosen. A majority of them was instructed by the towns to vote against the Constitution.

When the convention first met at Exeter on February 13, 1788, the Federalist members were shocked to find themselves in the minority. They moved to recess until June and conduct an active educational campaign. The motion narrowly carried, fifty-six to fifty-one.

The second session of the convention met at Concord, June 18 to 21. Between sessions a number of towns had reversed their positions, and a few delegates gave up their opposition. On June 21 a motion to ratify the Constitution was approved fifty-seven to forty-seven. Before that vote twelve proposed amendments were adopted, nine of them verbatim from those proposed by the Massachusetts state convention. Much of the opposition to the Constitution came from the central part of the state and isolated, agriculturally self-sufficient towns where small freeholders predominated. Those persons with mercantile interest, shipping and trading, security holders, and in the professions (law, medicine, and Congregational clergy) were mostly Federalists.

As the ninth state to ratify, New Hampshire completed the majority necessary to put the Constitution into effect!

USC-33.
Edmund Randolph, *A Letter of his excellency Edmund Randolph, esquire, on the Federal Constitution.* Richmond, October 10, 1787. [Richmond, 1787], 16 p. Caption title from page [4].

Richard O. Morris collection,
Lilly Library

Randolph, governor of Virginia and influential member of the Constitutional convention, was one of the three who refused to sign the completed document. While he called for a powerful central government, he believed the Constitution did not protect the interests of Virginia or provide enough safeguards for the rights of the people. He advocated state conventions that would recommend amendments to a second Constitutional convention. He believed that unless amended in this manner, the government would end in monarchy or aristocracy.

The letter was written to inform the Virginia legislature why he had not signed the Constitution, but only was made available to the public when published in this pamphlet form late in December 1787. One passage is very revealing:

> These were my opinions, while I acted as a Delegate; they sway me while I speak as a private citizen. I shall therefore cling to the union, as the rock of our salvation, and urge Virginia to finish the salutary work, which she has begun. And if after our best efforts for amendments they cannot be obtained. . . I will as an individual citizen, accept the constitution; because I would regulate myself by the spirit of America.

Publication of Randolph's letter was brought about by four members of the Virginia House of Delegates, as explained in two preliminary pages. It is not known if the pamphlet was printed with a title page, or who printed it.

The state convention met in Richmond, June 2-27, 1788, after the election of 170 delegates to represent counties, cities, towns, and corporations, including fourteen from the District of Kentucky. The merits and defects of the Constitution were debated with force, logic, eloquence, and bitterness by some of the best political minds in the state. Antifederalist leaders were Patrick Henry, George Mason, and Richard Henry Lee. Supporting the Constitution were James Madison, John Marshall, George Wythe, Edmund Randolph, and in private George Washington. Henry supported amendments prior to ratification, but his motion to that effect on June 25, was defeated 82 to 80. On the same day a motion to ratify passed 89 to 79, two delegates abstaining. On June 27 a committee reported twenty articles of a declaration of rights and twenty other proposed amendments that were agreed to by the convention. Ten were included in the federal Bill of Rights.

The fate of the Constitution in Virginia was of immense interest throughout the country, because it was the largest state and contained one-fifth of the country's population. Ratification doomed the hopes of Antifederalists in the remaining states which had not yet voted. Virginia became the tenth state to ratify the Constitution, following New Hampshire's pivotal vote a few days earlier.

To THE PRINTER.

SIR,

THE inclosed letter contains the reasons of his Excellency Governor Randolph for refusing his signature to the proposed Fœderal Constitution of Government submitted to the several states by the late Convention at Philadelphia. The manner in which we have obtained it, and the authority by which we convey it to the Public, through the channel of your Press, will be explained by the letter herewith sent to you, which, we request may precede his Excellency's letter to the Speaker of the House of Delegates in your publication of them.

M. SMITH,
CHARLES M. THRUSTON.
JOHN H. BRIGGS.
MANN PAGE, jun.

RICHMOND, 1787

USC-34.
Patrick Henry to Thomas
Madison, October 21, 1787.
Richmond. Autograph letter
signed, 2 p.

James S. Schoff collection,
Clements Library

Patrick Henry, five times governor of Virginia, was the most influential opponent of the Constitution in the state. Before a state convention had been authorized, he wrote to his brother-in-law about his attitude:

> For such is the Warmth of all Members of Assembly concerning the new Constitution that no kind of business can be done 'till that is considered, so far at least as to recommend a Convention of the People. Great Divisions are likely to happen & I am afraid for the Consequences. I can never agree to the proposed plan without Amendments, tho' many are willing to swallow [it] in its present form.

Approximately one-fifth of the reported debates in the state convention are given over to Henry's remarks. His primary objections were that the sovereignty of the states would be lost under the Constitution, and the rights of conscience, trial by jury, and liberty of the press were not secured. He also opposed the taxing power and control of the army granted to the central government.

USC-35.
Nathan Dane to Elbridge Gerry.
New York, June 12, 1788.
Autograph letter signed, 2 p.

Lilly Library

Dane opposed the Constitution in the debates of the Confederation Congress, September 1787, on transmitting it to the states. His later letter relates to the Virginia and New York conventions. Gerry had been a delegate to the Massachusets convention and refused to ratify the Constitution. Regarding the Virginia convention, Dane wrote:

> the debates began the 4th. no question taken indicative of Superiority on either side— agreed to go though the Constitution— the numbers were as nearly equal as possible— but Gov. Randolph to day declared in favor of adopting the Constitution— the district of Kentucky is against the Constitution— and if the 4 counties on the Ohio between the Pennsyla. line & Big Sandy Creek Join in the opposition the Constitution cannot be adopted. Nothing very material had occurred here [N.Y.]— it seems to be agreed by both parties in New York, that 46 members chosen are against the Constitution and 19 for it.

USC-36.
James Madison to George
Washington. Richmond June 25
[1788]. Autograph letter signed,
1 p.

Lilly Library

This letter is docketed in Washington's hand on the verso. At Mount Vernon he anxiously awaited the results of the Virginia convention that was debating the Constitution. Madison was a delegate to it and promptly sent his friend the good news:

> On the question today for *previous* amendments the vote stood 80 ays— 88 noes— On the final question the ratification passed 89 ays— 79 noes. Subsequent amendments will attend the act; but are yet to be settled. The temper of the minority will be better known tomorrow. The proceedings have been without flaw or pretext for it; and there is no doubt that acquiescence if not cordiality will be maintained by the unsuccessful party.

Dear Sir   Rich? Jan. 25.

On the question today for previous amend-
-ments. the votes stood 80 ays - 88 noes - on the final ques-
-tion the ratification passed 89 ays - 79 noes. Subsequent amend
-ments will attend the act; but are yet to be settled. The
temper of the minority will be better known tomorrow. The proceed-
-ings have been without flaw or pretext for it; and there
is no doubt that acquiescence if not cordiality will be mani-
-fested by the unsuccessful party. Two of the leaders however
betray the effect of the disappointment, so far as it is marked
in their countenances -   In haste yours

                                    Js Madison Jr

USC-37.

Debates and other proceedings of the Convention of Virginia, convened at Richmond on Monday the 2d day of June, 1788, for the purpose of deliberating on the Constitution recommended by the Grand Federal Convention. To which is prefixed the Federal Constitution. 3 volumes. The imprint on volume 1 reads: Petersburg: Printed by Hunter and Prentis. M,DCC,LXXXVIII [ie. 1788] The volume number is only indicated on Errata, p. 194. Volume II imprint reads: Petersburg: Printed by William Prentis. M,DCC,LXXXIX. Volume III imprint reads: Petersburg: Printed by William Prentis. M,DCC,LXXXIX. The volumes are separately paged.

Richard O. Morris collection,
Lilly Library

This record of the debates in the Virginia convention is the most complete of any of the state ratifying conventions. David Robertson, professional shorthand expert, was retained to record the proceedings. To understand clearly the positions of both the supporters and opponents of the Constitution, reference to these *Debates* is necessary. Some of the greatest political minds of the time were delegates to the convention, defending their views logically and sometimes brilliantly.

USC-38.

Henry Knox to Arthur St. Clair. New York, July 3, 1788. Autograph letter signed, 2 p.

Lilly Library

Secretary of War Knox wrote to St. Clair, just appointed Governor of the Northwest Territory, about the two recent state ratifications of the Constitution and the decision pending in New York:

> I rejoice my dear sir in having the pleasure of congratulating you on the adoption of the constitution by ten states. . . The Convention of this state [N.Y.] are setting— The Majority decidedly against it 44, to the minority of 19 in favor— We have not had time yet to know whether the adoption of New Hampshire and Virginia will make any alteration in the sentiments of the Majority. It is supposed otherwise— and that the Convention will stipulate for amendments previous to the adoption and then adjourn to a distant day— Congress will immediately pass the necessary acts for organizing the Constitution.

USC-39.
To the Tenants of the County of Albany, [Albany? 1788].
Broadside, 8 1/4 x 6 3/8.

See illustration on page 104

Lilly Library

This broadside, from a presumed tenant farmer, circulated in Albany County, New York, prior to the election for delegates to the state convention to consider the Constitution:

> If you wish the establishment of a national government with powers to usurp and destroy your constitutional rights and liberties;—Then go and give your votes for the establishment of this New Constitution. If you wish the proposed Constitution properly amended before it is adopted— Then let us join our interest in voting for such persons, whose sentiments and principles agree with our own.

On January 31, 1788, the House called for election of delegates April 29 - May 2, to meet in Poughkeepsie on June 17. The Senate concurred on February 1. When the results were tabulated, the Federalists had elected nineteen delegates, and the Antifederalists, forty-six for a total of sixty-five. But most of the delegates were in favor of increasing the power of the central government. The Federalists wanted to ratify the Constitution as it stood; the Antifederalists wanted amendments. The prolonged convention from June 17 to July 26 was primarily concerned with the wording of ratification, whether it should be conditional depending on amendments, or ratification followed by recommended amendments.

More than half of the debates were carried on between Alexander Hamilton, Federalist, and Melancton Smith, Antifederalist, although Robert Yates was the formal leader of the opposition. Compromises were made by both sides. In the end a form of ratification was agreed upon containing "explanatory" amendments, "recommendatory" amendments, and a circular letter to all the states calling for a second Constitutional convention. On July 26 the Constitution in this form was ratified by a vote of 30 to 27, the smallest margin of all the states except Rhode Island. New York was the eleventh state to ratify.

USC-40.
We the people of the United States, in order to form a more perfect union. . . [Poughkeepsie, N.Y., 1788.] Nicholas Power. Caption Title. 20 p.

See illustration on page 60

Clements Library

The Constitution is printed on one side only of the first seventeen leaves, followed by the documents submitting it to the states. It was published for the use of delegates to the New York convention. This copy belonged to Chancellor Robert R. Livingston, a member who was a staunch Federalist and a frequent speaker in the state convention.

To the Tenants of the County of Albany.

PERMIT a fellow tenant to address you in plain language, on the great importance of the next election for delegates in Convention.

I am an inhabitant of the county of Albany, and a tenant, My farm is subject to rents and services. These are moderate, nor do I complain that they are exacted with rigor; but such I believe are the natural effects of all tenures, that they produce a kind of dependence, for I have often given my assent to the will of my landlord in supporting his political importance, without enquiring into the propriety of it; nor do I now complain that I hold my farm under him, I inherit it as such, nor do I wish to invade the right or property of another, but to secure my own.

Time brings with it experience, and this has at last convinced me that my landlord has been, and may be *wrong* as well as others——That he may be for a mode of government very convenient for a great man, but not so for a common farmer; in fact, that he may have an interest to support, at the expence of my own, and that whatever be the event of our present contest, I know my rents will be demanded and that I must pay them: I know too, that in voting by ballot, neither my landlord nor any other person can find out how, or for whom I give my vote.

At the beginning of our troubles with Great-Britain, I was ignorant of my own rights—but the great men of America took pains to inform me in what they consisted. They told me that power in government originated with the people and that the Parliament of Great Britain had no right to tax us, because the people of America did not chuse them, this was self-evident; and, it convinced me that I had a right to oppose them. Under this firm persuasion, I steped forward at an early period, to defend my rights, against the British troops. During the long war I was often called into the field, and suffered with others the distresses incident to it. My family were poorly and coarsely cloathed—my sons grew up into manhood without any improvement but in the use of arms—the produce of my farm I freely parted with, to support our army: all this I bore with manly fortitude—My freedom, my farm, and the constitutional rights of my state are secured by the blessings of peace. But

our great and rich men are still unsatisfied---They want a new plan of Government----They have by writing, printing and harranging, endeavored to shew it to be good, and the danger if you do not adopt it—you have also heard the many objections which have been made against it----the subject is fairly before you, and I presume that you have read and well considered the arguments for and against it.

You now are to come forward to determine by your votes the fate of yourselves, and your posterity. and I thank kind Heaven, that the appeal is made to you.

If therefore you wish to exclude yourselves forever hereafter from voting for an executive and senate;

If you wish that the national government shall have the power, by a capitation or *poll*-tax, to rate the poor equal to the rich;

If you chuse to exclude yourselves in civil cases from a trial by jury;

If you wish a standing army in time of peace subject to the will of one man;

If you wish to be at the expence of following a cause upon an appeal to a far distant country;

If you will subject yourselves as militia-men to be called abroad to any state in the Union, under the command of continental officers;

If you chuse to double the expence of government;

If you wish the establishment of a national government with powers to usurp and destroy your constitutional rights and liberties;—Then *go* and give your votes for the establishment of this New Constitution.

But if, on the contrary, you, my fellow tenants, would retain your constitutional rights, and not surrender them to the will and pleasure of a few great and rich men;

If you wish the proposed Constitution properly amended before it is adopted—Then let us join our interest in voting for such persons, whose sentiments and principles agree with our own.

A TENANT.

USC-41.
[Alexander Hamilton,] *The Independent Journal: or the General Advertiser.* Saturday, October 27, 1787. "The FOEDERALIST No. I. To the people of the State of New York." 4 p.

Lilly Library

This newspaper contains the first appearance in print of the first of *The Federalist* essays. It was written by Alexander Hamilton, and by December 12 was reprinted in five New York newspapers and in one newspaper each in Massachusetts, Rhode Island, Pennsylvania, and Virginia.

Hamilton's intention was to persuade New York to ratify the Constitution. Ultimately he wrote fifty-one essays explaining and recommending the document. He was joined by James Madison, who wrote fourteen essays, and John Jay, who wrote five. Authorship of fifteen more, making a total of eighty-five are in doubt between Hamilton and Madison, although most of them have been assigned to Madison. Whatever influence they had on the ratification argument, *The Federalist Papers,* as they are also called, are considered a classic work of political theory. They expand on the nature of republican government and federalism, and still are respected. They have been reprinted in many editions and translated into several languages.

With the exception of the last eight numbers, all of the essays appeared first in New York newspapers before being reprinted outside the city. All of the essays were signed "Publius," adopted as a pseudonym.

USC-42.
The Federalist: a collection of essays, written in favor of the new Constitution, as agreed upon by the Federal Convention, September 17, 1787. New York: printed and sold by J. and A. M'Lean. M,DCC,LXXXVIII. 2 volumes.

The Newberry Library

A New York City committee working for the ratification of the Constitution commissioned John and Archibald M'Lean to publish *The Federalist* in pamphlet form. The "pamphlet," representing the first collected edition, ran to two volumes. Volume I was published May 22, 1788, and contained thirty-six essays; volume II was published May 28 and contained forty-nine essays, the last eight of which were appearing in print for the first time. The M'Leans printed 500 copies of each volume.

This copy once belonged to Thomas Jefferson and bears his customary initials of ownership: a "T" before the "J" printed on the signature, and a "J" after the "T" signature (on pages 97 and 217). On the front flyleaf of volume I Jefferson noted the essay numbers which he thought had been written by each of the three authors. In volume II he indicated only the numbers which he thought had been written by James Madison.

The volumes were widely circulated throughout the country. Just before the election of delegates to the New York convention, sixty copies of volume I were sent for distribution in Albany and Montgomery counties. Hamilton, at the request of Madison, sent fifty-two copies of volume I to Governor Edmund Randolph of Virginia, and later sent copies of volume II as well. Though the sale of the book may have been brisk for the times, the M'Leans had copies remaining after the ratification struggle was won. Some of the numbering was changed in the first collected edition from that used in the newspaper printings.

USC-43.
Observations leading to a fair examination of the system of government, proposed by the late Convention; and to several and essential and necessary alterations in it. In a number of letters from the Federal Farmer to the Republican. [New York, Thomas Greenleaf] Printed in the year M,DCC,LXXXCII. 40 p.

See illustration on page 93

Richard O. Morris collection,
Lilly Library

This pamphlet circulated in the state of New York beginning in November 1787. The author is not known, beyond the likelihood of his being a New Yorker. The addressee, "The Republican," may have been Governor George Clinton. The five letters, dated in October, were one of the superior Antifederalist publications.

The "Federal Farmer" said of the proposed Constitution: "It leaves the powers of government, and representation of the people, so unnaturally divided between the general and state governments, that the operations of our system must be very uncertain." He thought it would be difficult to frame a bill of rights for such a varied country, and that it was not possible for free and equal government to encompass such a large and heterogeneous territory.

USC-44.
[John Jay,] *An Address to the people of the state of New-York, on the Subject of the Constitution, agreed upon at Philadelphia, the 17th of September, 1787.* New York: printed by Samuel and John London, printers to the state. [1788]. 19 p.

Richard O. Morris collection,
Lilly Library

The essay is typesigned at the end: "A Citizen of New York." It was written in April 1788 while Jay was convalescing from an injury. He pointed out the weakness of the country under the Article of Confederation, defended the Constitution, and argued against a second convention to alter defects that were being designated by the Antifederalists. Jay repeated the Federalist argument that a bill of rights was unnecessary. He argued the Constitution be accepted as the best available frame of government. The dissatisfied could then work for amendments in the manner specified in Article V of the Constitution.

USC-45.
The debates and proceedings of the Convention of the state of New-York, assembled at Poughkeepsie, on the 17th June, 1788. To deliberate and decide on the form of Federal government, recommended by the General Convention at Philadelphia, on the 17th September, 1787. Taken in short-hand. New-York: printed and sold by Francis Childs. M,DCC,LXXXVIII. [2], ii, 144 p.

Richard O. Morris collection,
Lilly Library

Francis Childs, publisher of *The Daily Advertiser* (New York), took the shorthand notes of the debates through July 2, 1788; following that date he reported only summaries of the proceedings. The publication contains a list of the delegates by county represented, the recorded votes, and many of the major speeches. The preface is dated December 1, 1788; and the book is open to the recorded final vote on ratification, July 26.

USC-46.
Observations on the proposed Constitution for the United States of America, clearly showing it to be a complete system of aristocracy and tyranny, and destructive of the rights and liberties of the people. Printed in the State of New-York. M,DCC,LXXXVIII. [126] p.

An anthology of Antifederalist material used in the ratification struggle in New York state contains (1) reasons of dissent in Pennsylvania, (2) letter of Edmund Randolph, (3) Samuel Bryan's nine letters on the Constitution to the people of Pennsylvania, and (4) an appendix containing the Constitution. The Antifederalists in New York City had them prepared and sent to Albany for local use.

Bryan was one of the most censorious opponents of the Constitution. He criticized the secrecy of the Constitutional convention, the proposed powers of Congress, and the absence of a bill of rights. Members of the convention were declared to be conspirators. He thought Washington had been duped, and Franklin was too old to account for his actions. His essays were the most vituperative of any that circulated during the ratification argument.

USC-47.
[Melancton Smith,] *An Address to the people of the state of New York: showing the necessity of making amendments to the Constitution, proposed for the United States, previous to its adoption. By a Plebeian.* Printed in the State of New-York. M,DCC,LXXX,VIII. 26 p.

Smith, who was a merchant and lawyer, served the state of New York in the Confederation Congress, 1785-88. He represented Dutchess County in the state convention on ratification. A leading Antifederalist, he carried the brunt of the attack against the Constitution. In this pamphlet Smith urged amendments as a condition of ratification. The last four pages are a direct reply to John Jay's *Address* (item 44).

When he saw amendments could not be passed, he favored ratification with reservations. Finally convinced that neither conditions nor reservations were politically acceptable, he voted for ratification anyway.

USC-48.
Simeon Baldwin, *An oration pronounced before the citizens of New-Haven, July 4th, 1788, in commemoration of the Declaration of Independence and establishment of the Constitution of the United States of America.* New Haven: printed by J. Meigs. M,DCC,LXXXVIII. 16 p.

The twelfth anniversary of the Declaration of Independence combined with enough state ratifications of the Constitution to put it into effect aroused a special celebration on July 4, 1788, in several cities. Two are noted here.

Baldwin, a Yale graduate, lawyer, and judge, was the principal speaker at the celebration in New Haven. The observance was complete with a parade "near one mile and three quarters" made up of various tradesmen, the everpresent Federal ship and other floats, then dinner and an evening ball.

The speaker sought to dispel apprehensions about the new Constitution: "We have everything to hope— nothing to fear. The powers of Congress are solely directed to national objects."

USC-49.
Francis Hopkinson, *Order of Procession, in honor of the establishment of the Constitution of the United States. . .* Philadelphia: Printed by Hall and Sellers [1788]. Broadside, 13 x 14.
Clements Library

The celebration in Philadelphia on July 4, 1788, was the greatest in the nation. In anticipation of the ninth state's ratification, Judge Francis Hopkinson had assembled a committee to plan a joint celebration of the federal Union and the anniversary of independence. New Hampshire's ratification on June 21, was closely followed by Virginia on June 25 and led to a flurry of preparations.

The procession which wound its way through Philadelphia had some five thousand marchers. All the trades were represented, civil and military officials, the professions, students, and clergy. Charles Wilson Peale designed a gigantic float called "The Grand Federal Edifice," pulled along the line of the parade. It stood thirty-six feet high. Peale also supervised work on the "Federal Ship," thirty-three feet long, mounted with twenty guns. James Wilson gave his oration at Bush Hill to an estimated audience of 17,000 people—half the population of Philadelphia.

To line up this tremendous parade, nine "superintendents" supervised the assemblage, using broadside directions like this one. The parade started moving at nine-thirty in the morning, and the last of the marchers reached Bush Hill about one o'clock in the afternoon. Before eating, the crowd drank ten toasts. The report noted "No spirits or wines of any kind were introduced; American porter, beer and cyder were the only liquors."

USC-50.
Proceedings and debates of the convention of North Carolina, convened at Hillsborough, on Monday the 21st of July, 1788, for the purpose of deliberating and determining on the Constitution recommended by the general Convention at Philadelphia, the 17th day of September, 1787. To which is prefixed the said Constitution. Edenton: Printed by Hodge & Wills, printers to the state. MDCCLXXXIX. 280 p.
Richard O. Morris collection, Lilly Library

North Carolina was the first state to reject the Constitution. On December 7, 1787, the general assembly called for election of delegates, March 28-29, 1788, to meet at Hillsborough on July 21 to consider the Constitution. A heated and prolonged campaign resulted in a landslide victory for the Antifederalists. Delegates from the western counties were nearly unanimous in their objections. On August 2 a resolution "neither to ratify or reject the Constitution" passed the convention. Eleven states had ratified.

Supporters of the Constitution did not despair, but began a well-orchestrated campaign for a second convention. On November 30 the legislature called for a new election of delegates to a second convention to reconsider the Constitution. They were not elected until August 21-22, 1789. One hundred and two of the delegates had been members of the first convention. Of the 169 new delegates, 135 were Federalists. They met at Fayetteville on November 16. Five days later they voted to ratify the Constitution 194 to 77.

Citizens of North Carolina had watched the new government function under the Constitution without the disasters predicted by some Antifederalists. Amendments in the form of a Bill of Rights had passed Congress and were in process of being ratified by the states.

Order of Procession,

In honor of the establishment of the Constitution of the United States.

To parade precisely at Eight o'Clock in the Morning, of FRIDAY, the 4th of JULY, 1788, proceeding along Third-street to Callowhill-street; thence to Fourth-street; down Fourth-street to Market-street; thence to the Grounds in Front of Bush-hill.

I.
MAJOR *Pancake*, with twelve Axe-men, in frocks and caps.

II.
The City Troop of Light-Horse, commanded by Colonel *Miles*.

III.
INDEPENDENCE.
John Nixon, Esq; on horseback, bearing the staff and cap of Liberty—The words, " 4th July, 1776," in gold letters, pendant from the staff.

IV.
Four Pieces of Artillery, with a detachment from the Train, commanded by Captains *Morrell* and *Fisher*.

V.
ALLIANCE WITH FRANCE.
Thomas Fitzsimons, Esq; on horseback, carrying a flag, white ground, having three fleurs-de lys and thirteen stars in union, over the words " 6th February, 1778," in gold letters.

VI.
Corps of Light-Infantry, commanded by Capt. *Claypoole*, from the 1st regiment.

VII.
DEFINITIVE TREATY OF PEACE.
George Clymer, Esq; on horseback, carrying a staff, adorned with olive and laurel, the words " 3d September, 1783," in gold letters, pendant from the staff.

VIII.
Col. *John Shee*, on horseback, carrying a flag, blue field, with a laurel and an olive wreath over the words—" WASHINGTON, THE FRIEND OF HIS COUNTRY!" in silver letters—the staff adorned with olive and laurel.

IX.
The City Troop of Light Dragoons, commanded by Major *W. Jackson*.

X.
Richard Bache, Esq; on horseback, as a Herald, attended by a trumpet, proclaiming a New Æra—the words " NEW ÆRA," in gold letters, pendant from the Herald's staff, and the following lines,
Peace o'er our land her olive wand extends,
And white rob'd Innocence from Heaven descends;
The crimes and frauds of Anarchy shall fail,
Returning Justice lifts again her scale.

XI.
The Hon. *Peter Muhlenberg*, Esq; Vice-President of Pennsylvania, on horseback, carrying a flag, blue field, emblazoned—the words " 17th September, 1787," in silver letters, on the flag.

XII.
Band of Music.

XIII.
The Honorable Chief-Justice M'Kean,
The Hon. Judge Atlee, The Hon. Judge Rush, (in their Robes of Office.)
In an ornamented Car, drawn by six horses, bearing the CONSTITUTION, framed, fixed on a staff, crowned with the Cap of Liberty—the words—" THE PEOPLE," in gold letters, on the staff, immediately under the Constitution.

XIV.
Corps of Light-Infantry, commanded by Capt. *Hysham*, from the 3d regiment.

XV.
Ten Gentlemen, representing the States that have adopted the Fœderal Constitution, viz.
1. *Duncan Ingraham*, Esq; — New-Hampshire.
2. *Jonathan Williams*, jun. Esq; — Massachusetts.
3. *Jared Ingersoll*, Esq; — Connecticut.
4. Hon. Chief Justice *Brearley*, — New-Jersey.
5. *James Wilson*, Esq; — Pennsylvania.
6. Col. *Thomas Robinson*, — Delaware.
7. Hon. *J. E. Howard*, Esq; — Maryland.
8. Col. *Febiger*, — Virginia.
9. *W. Ward Burrows*, Esq; — South-Carolina.
10. *George Meade*, Esq; — Georgia.
Bearing distinguishing flags and walking arm in arm, emblematic of Union.

XVI.
Colonel *William Williams*, in armour, on horseback, bearing a Shield, emblazoned with the arms of the United States.

XVII.
The Montgomery county Troop of Light-Horse, commanded by *James Morris*, Esquire.

XVIII.
An ornamented Car, drawn by four horses, bearing Captain *Thomas Bell*, carrying the Flag of The United States,—Monsieur *Barbé de Marbois*, Flag of France,—Mr. *Heineken*, Flag of The United Netherlands,—Mr. *Holstead*, Flag of Sweeden,—Mr. *Secke*, Flag of Prussia,—*Thomas Barclay*, Esquire, Flag of Morocco,—States in alliance with America.

XIX.
The Judge, Register, Marshal, and other Officers of the Court of Admiralty, with their insignia.

XX.
Wardens of the Port, and Tonnage Officers.

XXI.
Collector of the Customs, and Naval Officer.

XXII.
The Surveyor-General, Receiver-General, Secretary, and other Officers of the Land Office.

XXIII.
Register, Recorder of Deeds, and Comptroller-General.

XXIV.
Peter Baynton, Esq; and Colonel *Isaac Melcher*, as an American and an Indian, smoking the Calumet of Peace, in a carriage drawn by two horses.

XXV.
GRAND FŒDERAL EDIFICE, on a carriage drawn by ten horses, containing Messrs. *Hilary Baker*, *George Latimore*, *John Wharton*, *John Nesbitt*, *Samuel Morris*, *John Brown*, *Tench Francis*, *Joseph Anthony*, *John Chaloner* and *Peter J——t*, citizens of the Union—
Attended by the House-carpenters.

XXVI.
Corps of Light Infantry, commanded by Captain *Rose*, 5th regiment.

XXVII.
The Agricultural Society, headed by their President, *S. Powel*, Esq;

XXVIII.
The Farmers, headed by *Richard Peters*, *Richard Willing*, *Samuel Meredith*, *Isaac Warner*, *George Gray*, *William Pelen*,——*Burkhart* and *Charles Willing*, with ploughs, &c.

XXIX.
The Manufacturing Society, with the spinning and carding machines, looms, &c. headed by *Robert Hare*, Esq;

Corps of Light Infantry, commanded by Capt. *Robinson*, from the 6th regiment.

The Marine Society, with their insignia.

The Fœderal Ship, The UNION, commanded by *John Green*, Esq; Captain *S. Smith*, *W. Belcher* and Mr. *Mercer*, Lieutenants, with a proper crew of Officers and Seamen.

The Pilots of the Port, with a Pilot Boat.

Boat Builders, with a Barge.

The Ship-carpenters, Sail-makers, Rope-makers, Block-makers and Riggers.

The Merchants and Traders of the city and liberties of Philadelphia, headed by *Thomas Willing*, Esq; with their insignia—followed by the Merchants Clerks.

Corps of Light Infantry, commanded by Capt. *Sproat*, from the 4th regiment.

TRADES and PROFESSIONS.

XXX.
1. Cordwainers.

XXXI.
2. Coach-painters.

XXXII.
3. Cabinet and Chair-makers.

XXXIII.
4. Brick-makers.

XXXIV.
5. Painters.

XXXV.
6. Porters.

XXXVI.
7. Watch-makers.

XXXVII.
8. Fringe and Ribband Weavers.

XXXVIII.
9. Bricklayers.

XXXIX.
10. Taylors.

XL.
11. Instrument-makers, Turners and Windsor Chair-makers.

XLI.
12. Carvers and Gilders.

XLII.
13. Coopers.

XLIII.
14. Plane-makers.

XLIV.
15. Whip Manufacturers.

XLV.
16. Black-smiths, White-smiths, Nail-smiths and Bell-hangers.

XLVI.
17. Coach-makers.

XLVII.
18. Potters.

XLVIII.
19. Hatters.

XLIX.
20. Wheel-wrights.

L.
21. Tin-plate Workers.

LI.
22. Skinners, Breeches-makers and Glovers.

LII.
23. Tallow-chandlers.

LIII.
24. Butchers.

LIV.
25. Printers, Stationers and Book-binders.

LV.
26. Saddlers.

LVI.
27. Stone-cutters.

LVII.
28. Bakers.

LVIII.
29. Gun-smiths.

LIX.
30. Copper-smiths.

LX.
31. Gold-smiths, Silver-smiths and Jewellers.

LXI.
32. Distillers.

LXII.
33. Tobacconists.

LXIII.
34. Brass-founders.

LXIV.
35. Stocking Manufacturers.

LXV.
36. Curriers and Tanners.

LXVI.
37. Druggists.

LXVII.
38. Upholsterers.

LXVIII.
39. Sugar-refiners.

LXIX.
40. Brewers.

LXX.
41. Peruke-makers and Barbers.

LXXI.
42. Ship-chandlers.

LXXII.
43. Engravers.

LXXIII.
44. Plaisterers.

Corps of Light Infantry, commanded by Capt. *Rees*, from the 2d regiment.

The Civil and Military Officers of Congress in the City.

His Excellency the PRESIDENT, and the SUPREME EXECUTIVE COUNCIL.

The Justices of the Common Pleas and the Magistrates.

Sheriff and Coroner, on horseback.

City Wardens.

Constables and Watchmen.

The gentlemen of the Bar, headed by the Honorable *Edward Shippen*, Esquire, President of the Common Pleas, and *William Bradford*, Esquire, Attorney-General, followed by the students of Law.

The Clergy of the different denominations.

The College of Physicians, headed by their President, Dr. *Redman*.

Students of the University, headed by the Vice-Provost, and of other Schools, headed by their respective Principals, Professors, Masters and Tutors.

The County Troop of Light Horse, commanded by Major *W. Macpherson*, bringing up the rear of the whole.

Major *Fullerton* to attend the right wing——Colonel *Mentges* the left wing.

On the UNION GREEN, at Bush-hill, Mr. WILSON will deliver an Oration, suited to the day; after which a Collation will be prepared for the company.

The following gentlemen, distinguished by a white feather in the hat, are Superintendants of the procession. General *Mifflin*, General *Stewart*, Colonel *Proctor*, Colonel *Gurney*, Major *Moore*, Major *Lenox*, Mr. *Peter Brown*, Colonel *Will*, Colonel *Marsh*.

To add to the entertainment of the day, ten vessels will be prepared and paraded as follows, one representing *New-Hampshire*, opposite the Northern-Liberties,—the next for *Massachusetts*, opposite Vine-street,—*Connecticut*, opposite Race-street,—*New-Jersey*, Arch—*Pennsylvania*, Market—*Delaware*, Chesnut—*Maryland*, Walnut—*Virginia*, Spruce—*South-Carolina*, Pine—and *Georgia*, South-street. The RISING SUN, under the command of Captain *Philip Brown*, will be anchored off Market street, and superbly dressed. At night she will be handsomely illuminated.

By Order of the Committee of Arrangement,
Francis Hopkinson, Chairman.

Philadelphia: Printed by HALL and SELLERS.

USC-51.
New York, *Gazette of the United States.* Saturday, December 5, 1789, 4 p.

Lilly Library

IMPORTANT NEWS!
By the arrival of a Packet, in five days from Wilmington, North Carolina, we have received the agreeable intelligence that the Convention of that State ADOPTED THE NEW CONSTITUTION, on the 20th ult.

For the adoption. . .	193
Against it. . .	75
Majority. . .	118

The newspaper was in error on the date and the vote. The Constitution was ratified November 21, and the official vote was 194 to 77, a majority of 117.

USC-52.
September, 1789. At the General Assembly of the Governor and company of the State of Rhode Island, and Providence-plantations. . . [Providence: printed by Bennett Wheeler. 1789]. 28 p. Signed on p. 28 by Henry Ward, secretary of state.

Lilly Library

"An Act relative to a Convention in this State" was sent to the freemen of the towns "for the purpose of giving Instructions to their Representatives respecting the Appointment of a State Convention, for the purpose of considering and determining on said Constitution."

This was the second referendum on a convention in the state. A large majority of the town meetings instructed their representatives to vote against a convention. When the legislature reconvened after the referendum, a motion to authorize a convention was defeated 39 to 17.

See item 58 for subsequent action.

USC-53.
By the United States in Congress assembled, September 13, 1788, resolved that the first Wednesday in January next, be the day for appointing electors in the several states. . . that the first Wednesday in February next, be the day for the electors to assemble in their respective states, and vote for a President. . . [New York, 1788]. Broadside, 12 5/8 x 8.

Lilly Library

This election ordinance, passed by the Confederation Congress in New York City, explained the initial steps in formation of the new government under the Constitution. January 7, 1789, was the date set for the Electors to be selected, and February 4 for the Electors to cast ballots for a President. March 4 was the time "for commencing Proceedings under the said Constitution."

But on the designated day for the first Congress to meet, only a quarter of the members were present. It was April 1 before the House had a quorum and April 6 before the Senate could organize. Two hundred copies of this broadside were ordered printed. Charles Thomson, secretary to the Congress, signed those sent to the governors of the states. Members of Congress sent the document to state officials and friends.

By the United States in Congress assembled,

SEPTEMBER 13, 1788.

WHEREAS the Convention affembled in Philadelphia, purfuant to the Refolution of Congrefs of the 21ft February, 1787, did, on the 17th of September in the fame year, report to the United States in Congrefs affembled, a Conftitution for the People of the United States ; whereupon Congrefs, on the 28th of the fame September, did refolve unanimoufly, " That the faid report, with the Refolutions and Letter accompanying the fame, be tranfmitted to the feveral Legiflatures, in order to be fubmitted to a Convention of Delegates chofen in each State by the people thereof, in conformity to the Refolves of the Convention made and provided in that cafe:" And whereas the Conftitution fo reported by the Convention, and by Congrefs tranfmitted to the feveral Legiflatures, has been ratified in the manner therein declared to be fufficient for the eftablifhment of the fame, and fuch Ratifications duly authenticated have been received by Congrefs, and are filed in the Office of the Secretary---therefore,

RESOLVED, That the firft Wednefday in January next, be the day for appointing Electors in the feveral States, which before the faid day fhall have ratified the faid Conftitution; that the firft Wednefday in February next, be the day for the Electors to affemble in their refpective States, and vote for a Prefident; and that the firft Wednefday in March next, be the time, and the prefent Seat of Congrefs the place for commencing Proceedings under the faid Conftitution.

USC-54.
Wm. Smith D.D. to James Wilson, Esq. Chester, Kent County, Maryland. Jany 19th, 1789. Autograph letter signed, 3 p.
Lilly Library

Smith, a Scottish-born Anglican clergyman and educator, was at this time president of Washington College in Kent County, Maryland, and rector of Chester parish. A political gadfly, Smith was concerned here over the first federal elections for President and Vice-President. Because electors could not stipulate a vote for either office, the person intended for Vice-President might end up with more votes than the one wanted for President. This possibility was remedied by the twelfth Amendment in 1804 that allowed electors to name the President voted for, and the Vice-President voted for.

The possibility of a tie vote was not precluded initially, when the contest would be decided by the House of Representatives, as happened in 1800. The rival candidates for President were Thomas Jefferson and Aaron Burr, and the House chose Jefferson.

USC-55.
George Washington to John Langdon, Esq., Mount Vernon. April 14, 1789. Autograph letter signed, 1 p.
Lilly Library

Counting the electoral votes was the first task after the first Congress was organized. John Langdon, senator from New Hampshire, had been elected president *pro tempore* to perform this function. On April 6, 1789, before the members of both houses of Congress, Langdon personally opened, counted, and declared the results: for President, George Washington; for Vice-President, John Adams.

Washington was the nation's choice long before the election was held. He was indispensable in the experiment in self-government. Political scheming and maneuvering centered around the selection of the first Vice-President. John Adams received one less than a majority of the votes cast, but was second to Washington and therefore was declared elected.

The Senate then made arrangements officially to notify both men. Charles Thomson, longtime secretary to the Congress, was selected to carry the formal certification of election and a personal letter from Langdon to Washington, dated New York, April 6. Langdon wrote that the election was unanimous. "Suffer me, Sir, to indulge the hope that so auspicious a mark of public confidence will meet your approbation, and be considered a sure pledge of the affection and support you are to expect from a free and enlightened people."

Washington's reply was brief and to the point:

> Sir,
> I had the honor to receive your official Communication, by the hand of Mr. Secretary Thompson [Thomson], about one o'clock this day. Having concluded to obey the important & flattering call of my Country, and having been impressed with the idea of the expediency of my being with Congress at as early a period as possible; I propose to commence my journey on Thursday morning which will be the day after tomorrow.

Washington left Mount Vernon on April 16 and arrived in New York in the afternoon of April 23. The journey was marked by a varied but continuous ovation along the route. Never before had such an outpouring of affection, trust, and respect been shown to an American.

Mount Vernon April 14. 1789.

Sir,

      I had the honor to receive your official communication, by the hand of Mr Secretary Thompson, about one o'clock this day. — Having concluded to obey the important & flattering call of my Country, and having been impressed with an idea of the expediency of my being with Congress at as early a period as possible; I propose to commence my Journey on Thursday morning which will be the day after tomorrow. —

      I have the honor to be with sentiments of esteem Sir

      Your most Obed.t Serv.t

      G.º Washington

The Hon.ble
Mr Langdon Esq.r

USC-56.
New London. *Supplement to the Connecticut Gazette,* Friday, May 8, 1789. Broadside, 8 x 11.
See illustration on page 95
Lilly Library

This newspaper account of the first inauguration of a President on April 30, 1789, is dated May 1 at New York. At noon George Washington was escorted by a military procession from his residence on Cherry Street to Federal Hall. The oath prescribed by the Constitution (Article II, Section 1) was administered by Chancellor Robert R. Livingston of New York in the gallery fronting on Wall Street. Following the oath, Washington delivered his inaugural address to Congress in the Senate Chamber.

After the address: "His Excellency, accompanied by the Vice-President, the Speaker of the House of Representatives, and both Houses of Congress, then went to [St.] Paul's chapel, where divine service was performed by the Right Rev. Dr. Provost, Bishop of the Episcopal church in this State and Chaplain to Congress."

The newspaper account concluded on a note of optimism: "Every honest man must feel a singular felicity in contemplating this day. Good government, the best of blessings, now commences under favourable auspices. We beg leave to congratulate our readers on the great event."

USC-57.
Acts passed at the Congress of the United States of America, begun and held at the city of New York, on Wednesday the fourth of March, in the year MDCCLXXXIX. And of the independence of the United States, the thirteenth. Being the Acts passed at the first session of the First Congress of the United States. . . New York: printed by Francis Childs and John Swaine, printers to the United States. [1789]. XIV, [15]-93 [1], XCV-CV p.
Lilly Library

Shown here are the twelve proposed amendments to the Constitution as passed by the first United States Congress, and submitted to the states for ratification. The first proposal related to apportionment of legislators, the second to the pay of congressmen. They were not ratified by the states. The rest of them were ratified between November 1789 and December 1791, and became the first ten amendments, commonly called the Bill of Rights, to the Constitution. In general they guard the liberties of individuals against the abuse of national power.

James Madison pressed and managed the amendments in the House of Representatives, both to make good his campaign promises and to obviate any need for a second national convention. House approval was given to seventeen amendments. Senate approval was given to twelve of them. Action was completed on September 25, 1789. The amendments did not represent structural changes in the Constitution, but were supplemental to and a reinforcement of the document. They satisfied most of the critics of the Constitution.

CONGRESS of the UNITED STATES, begun and held at the city of New-York, on Wednesday the fourth of March, one thousand seven hundred and eighty-nine.

The Conventions of a number of the States having at the time of their adopting the Constitution expressed a desire, in order to prevent misconstruction or abuse of its powers, that further declaratory and restrictive clauses should be added: And as extending the ground of public confidence in the government will best insure the beneficent ends of its institution—

RESOLVED, by the Senate and House of Representatives of the United States of America in Congress assembled, two thirds of both Houses concurring, that the following articles be proposed to the legislatures of the several states, as amendments to the constitution of the United States, all or any of which articles, when ratified by three fourths of the said legislatures, to be valid to all intents and purposes, as part of the said constitution, viz.

ARTICLES in Addition to, and Amendment of, the CONSTITUTION OF THE UNITED STATES OF AMERICA, proposed by Congress, and ratified by the legislatures of the several states, pursuant to the fifth article of the original constitution.

Article the First.

After the first enumeration required by the first article of the constitution, there shall be one representative for every thirty thousand, until the number shall amount to one hundred, after which the proportion shall be so regulated by Congress, that there shall be not less than one hundred representatives, nor less than one representative for every forty thousand persons, until the number of representatives shall amount to two hundred; after which the proportion shall be so regulated by Congress, that there shall not be less than two hundred representatives, nor more than one representative for every fifty thousand persons.

Article the Second.

No law varying the compensation for the services of the Senators and Representatives, shall take effect, until an election of Representatives shall have intervened.

Article the Third.

Congress shall make no law respecting an establishment of religion, or prohibiting the free exercise thereof, or abridging the freedom of speech, or of the press; or the right of the people peaceably to assemble, and to petition the government for a redress of grievances.

Article the Fourth.

A well regulated militia being necessary to the security of a free state, the right of the people to keep and bear arms shall not be infringed.

Article the Fifth.

No soldier shall in time of peace be quartered in any house without the consent of the owner; nor in time of war, but in a manner to be prescribed by law.

Article the Sixth.

The right of the people to be secure in their persons, houses, papers, and effects, against unreasonable searches and seizures, shall not be violated; and no warrants shall issue, but upon probable cause, supported by oath or affirmation, and particularly describing the place to be searched, and the persons or things to be seized.

Article the Seventh.

No person shall be held to answer for a capital, or otherwise infamous crime, unless on a presentment or indictment of a Grand Jury, except in cases arising in the land or naval forces, or in the militia when in actual service in time of war or public danger; nor shall any person be subject for the same offence to be twice put in jeopardy of life or limb; nor shall be compelled in any criminal case, to be a witness against himself, nor be deprived of life, liberty or property, without due process of law; nor shall private property be taken for public use without just compensation.

Article the Eighth.

In all criminal prosecutions the accused shall enjoy the right to a speedy and public trial, by an impartial jury of the state and district wherein the crime shall have been committed, which district shall have been previously ascertained by law, and to be informed of the nature and cause of the accusation; to be confronted with the witnesses against him; to have compulsory process for obtaining witnesses in his favor, and to have the assistance of counsel for his defence.

Article the Ninth.

In suits at common law, where the value in controversy shall exceed twenty dollars, the right of trial by jury, shall be preserved, and no fact, tried by a Jury, shall be otherwise re-examined in any court of the United States, than according to the rules of the common law.

Article the Tenth.

Excessive bail shall not be required, nor excessive fines imposed, nor cruel and unusual ~~impeachments~~ *punishments* inflicted.

Article the Eleventh.

The enumeration in the constitution, of certain rights, shall not be construed to deny or disparage others retained by the people.

Article the Twelfth.

The powers not delegated to the United States by the constitution, nor prohibited by it to the states, are reserved to the states respectively, or to the people.

FREDERICK AUGUSTUS MUHLENBERG,
Speaker of the House of Representatives.

JOHN ADAMS, *Vice-President of the United States, and President of the Senate.*

ATTEST. JOHN BECKLEY, *Clerk of the House of Representatives.*
SAMUEL A. OTIS, *Secretary of the Senate.*

A 2

USC-57

USC-58.
June, 1790. At the General Assembly of the Governor and company of the state of Rhode-Island and Providence-Plantations. . . [Providence: printed by John Carter. 1790]. 16 p. Caption title.

See illustration on page 96

Lilly Library

The calling of a convention to consider the Constitution was defeated in the Rhode Island General Assembly eleven times over the course of twenty-three months. On January 17, 1790, the General Assembly finally approved a call, and delegates were elected on February 8 to meet at South Kingstown on March 1. The Constitution was debated clause by clause, and a special committee prepared a declaration of rights and twenty-one proposed amendments. On March 6 the convention adjourned to refer its proceedings to the freemen. The second session of the convention met at Newport on May 24, and on May 29 the Constitution was reluctantly ratified by a vote of 34 to 32. The margin of two votes was narrower than in any of the twelve states which had previously ratified, but Rhode Island acted after Congress threatened her with exclusion from commercial intercourse.

Seventeen days later, June 15, 1790, the state ratified eleven of the proposed amendments before the Congress.

USC-59.
Gilbert Stuart, "George Washington." [1796]. Oil painting, 36 5/16 x 32.

See illustration on page 76

Indiana University, Lilly House

Gilbert Charles Stuart (1755-1828), one of America's foremost portrait painters, was born in Rhode Island and moved to London in 1776 to study under Benjamin West. He opened studios in London and Dublin before returning to the United States. Anticipating an opportunity to paint a portrait of Washington, Stuart moved from New York to Philadelphia in 1795, where his work was in such demand that he delayed a year in approaching Washington about a sitting. Bearing a letter of introduction from John Jay, Stuart persuaded a reluctant Washington to sit for his portrait. Stuart faced a formidable task of bringing life to Washington's "stern, imperial face." While Stuart was personally not pleased with the painting, it received high praise when exhibited. Stuart painted fifteen copies of the portrait, known as the Vaughan type, showing the right side of Washington's face. Stuart later destroyed the original of this painting.

Washington agreed to two other sessions with Stuart, during which the Lansdowne type, full-length panting, and the Anthenaeum portrait, perhaps the best known, were produced.

This portrait was purchased by Eli Lilly of Indianapolis in 1940 from the descendants of John Jacob Astor. Astor, one of the richest entrepreneurs of his day, asked Stuart for the Washington painting during his own sitting for the portraitist. Mr. Lilly presented the painting to Indiana University along with his home. At the time Lilly acquired the portrait, it was described as "really a whole collection in one painting, a portrait of the greatest American citizen, by the greatest American artist, done for the richest American of his day."